Bible Promises, Prayers & Puzzles

Devotions to inspire...
Puzzles, quizzes & crosswords
for challenging fun!

Bible Promises, Prayers & Puzzles
©Product Concept Mfg., Inc.

Bible Promises, Prayers & Puzzles
ISBN 978-09963868-2-1

Published by Product Concept Mfg., Inc.
2175 N. Academy Circle #200, Colorado Springs, CO 80909

©2014 Product Concept Mfg., Inc. All rights reserved.

Written and Compiled by Patricia Mitchell
in association with Product Concept Mfg., Inc.

All scripture quotations are from the King James version
of the Bible unless otherwise noted.

Scriptures taken from the Holy Bible,
New International Version®, NIV®.
Copyright © 1973, 1978, 1984 by Biblica, Inc.™
Used by permission of Zondervan.
All rights reserved worldwide.
www.zondervan.com

Sayings not having a credit listed are contributed by writers
for Product Concept Mfg., Inc. or in a rare case,
the author is unknown.

All Rights Reserved. Except for brief quotes used in
reviews, articles, or other media, no part of this book
may be reproduced or transmitted in any form or by
any means, electronic or mechanical, including
photocopying, recording, or by information or
retrieval system, without permission by the publisher.

Bible Promises, Prayers & Puzzles

What is the use of having FAITH?
It is to connect the soul with God.

Henry Drummond

Everyone needs a little inspiration...and a little fun, too! So here's a book that combines both. Short, upbeat readings provide encouragement, inspiration, and a positive thought to brighten your day. The readings offer practical ways you can apply some of the Bible's timeless truths to your life, along with a short prayer of blessing and gratitude.

Each reading is paired with a puzzle that reflects the topic. It might be a themed crossword puzzle, multiple choice quiz, match-up, word search, or word game. Many puzzles will bring to mind familiar Bible people and places, while some could nudge you to think more deeply about God's love and His promises to you. And there are those that are included just to bring a smile.

Sit back with pencil in hand and enjoy the time you spend with *Bible Promises, Prayers & Puzzles*.

WHERE ARE YOU, GOD?

Where's God in all this? It's a natural question, given everything that's going on in the world. We hear about one shocking development after another, and sometimes the stories hit uncomfortably close to home. So where's God?

God is right where He always has been from the beginning of time. He has not abandoned us! There is faith, joy, love, and peace in the hearts of those who love Him. There is goodness and gratitude, selflessness and kindness all around you.

Take time to see Him in the words and actions of others. Find ways to be His heart and hands today.

Dear God, thank You for assuring me of Your presence.

Signs, Symbols, and Astonishing Sights

In the Bible, God proved His presence among people in many ways. Here are just a few of them!

ACROSS

1 God spoke to him in a burning bush
4 Angel Gabriel brought God's message to this young girl
5 God visited 10 plagues upon this nation to reveal His power
8 Abraham and Sarah's late-in-life son
10 God spoke to him in a still, small voice
12 Confusion of languages tower
13 Event that proved Jesus' victory over death
17 God put a star in the sky to lead them
18 Zechariah and Elizabeth's late-in-life son
19 God created this garden for Adam and Eve
20 God prepared a great fish to swallow this reluctant prophet

DOWN

2 Lot's wife turned into a pillar of __
3 God gave him the power to interpret the handwriting on the wall

DOWN Con't

6 Jesus walked on the water on this sea
7 Holy Spirit appeared as this at Jesus' baptism
9 God gave him the power to defeat Goliath
11 God gave him the power to crumble Jericho's walls
14 God told him to build an ark to survive the Flood
15 Holy Spirit appeared as tongues of __ at Pentecost
16 Along with five loaves and two of these, Jesus fed 5000
17 God sent this from heaven to feed the Children of Israel as they wandered in the desert

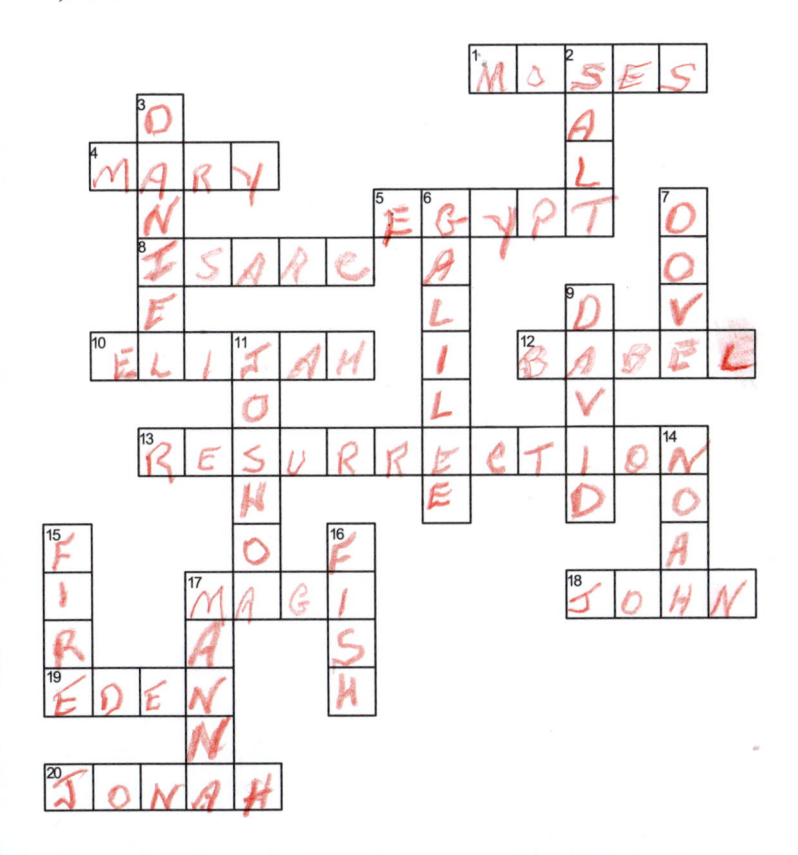

Crossword answers (as filled in)

- 1 Across: MOSES
- 3 Down: DANIEL
- 4 Across: MARY
- 5 Across: EGYPT
- 7 Down: DOVE
- 8 Across: ISAAC
- 9 Down: DAVID
- 10 Across: ELIJAH
- 11 Down: JOSHUA
- 12 Across: BABEL
- 13 Across: RESURRECTION
- 14 Down: NOAH
- 15 Down: FIRE
- 16 Down: FISH
- 17 Across: MAGI
- 18 Across: JOHN
- 19 Across: EDEN
- 20 Across: JONAH

SKY'S THE LIMIT

A leisurely hike in the woods or stroll along a garden path may not be in your plans today. You might not get a chance to gaze out at the sea or ponder a gorgeous sunset. But that doesn't mean you can't enjoy nature.

Simply go to the window, look up, and really see the sky. The broad, spacious, and ever-changing sky is just one of God's many natural wonders right where you are. Watch the clouds. Bask in the sunshine or listen to the rain. Maybe do a little star-gazing tonight, and let your imagination soar.

No matter where you are, let your heart give thanks for all creation!

Thank You, Lord, for the beauty of all creation!

All Creation

Many of the answers in this puzzle are related to the wonders of nature.

ACROSS

1 Physician, for short
4 Wing
5 Like rain
6 Ear in the field
9 Winter scene feature
13 Genetic code
14 Moon descriptor
15 Watch out for
17 Eve's garden
18 Most importantly (Abbr.)
20 Stretch to make do
21 Grain

DOWN

1 Daybreak
2 Stadium shout
3 Tigers, for example
6 Des Moines summer hour
7 Single
8 Fled
10 Wordless "yes"
11 Miner's goal
12 Compass point
16 Garden eaters, sometimes
17 Fencing sword
19 Heavens

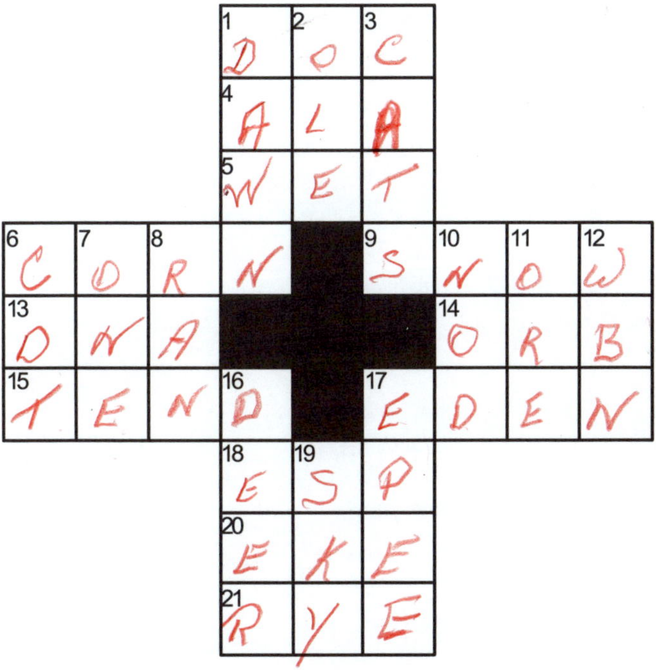

RELAX. HE'S GOT EVERYTHING UNDER CONTROL

When you're looking for answers to life's deepest questions, where do you go?

For many of us, public opinion, the Internet, what our friends say, or our own imagination is the go-to source for answers. But each answer we come up with is based on human perception, which is limited. There's just so much our eyes can see, our mind can absorb, our understanding can embrace. That's why, for the really important questions, God is the only reliable source. Always has been, always will be.

When you need an answer, ask Him the question. When you're looking for guidance, go to the One who has the knowledge, and the will and power to respond to your deepest needs.

Dear God, fill my heart and mind with Your peace, because I know that You are the answer.

True or False?

Here's a fun way to test what you know about truths God teaches in the words of Scripture.

1. T **(F)** There are many paths to God. (John 14:6)
2. **(T)** F God created everything that exists. (Hebrews 3:4)
3. **(T)** F Jesus has prepared a place in heaven for each one who believes in Him. (John 14:2)
4. T **(F)** When someone offends us, we should quickly publicize our side of the story. (Matthew 18:15 NIV)
5. T **(F)** God keeps a list of all the sins you have ever committed. (Psalm 130:3-4 NIV)
6. T **(F)** Certain people don't deserve our forgiveness. (Luke 6:37)
7. T **(F)** You can love God, yet not obey guidelines in the Bible that you find unreasonable or difficult to follow. (John 14:15)
8. **(T)** F Self-control is a result of the Holy Spirit's work in the believer. (Galatians 5:22-23 NIV)
9. T **(F)** If your enemy suffers, it serves him right; you don't need to lift a finger to help him. (Romans 12:20)
10. **(T)** F When you think about God's Word and meditate on what He says, your faith grows and strengthens. (Colossians 3:16)
11. **(T)** F There's no limit to what God can do. (Luke 1:37)

WHY WORRY?

Health. Finances. **Relationships**. What's **happening** now. What might happen in the future. There's a lot to **worry** about, and most of us do. But God tells us not to worry, and for a very **practical reason**: so much of what worries us, we have no **power** to **affect** one way or the other! "Who of you by worrying can add a **single hour** to your life?" Jesus asked His **disciples**. "Since you cannot do this very **little thing**, why do you worry about the rest?" (Luke 12:25-26 niv).

The **time** we spend worrying **clouds** our **thinking** and **prevents** us from doing what's within our **control**, such as **adopting** healthy habits of **mind** and **body**; making sound **financial** decisions; **treating** others the way we want to be treated; **responding** wisely to **events** that touch our lives; leaving the future in **God's hands**. All this is **enough** to keep any of us too **busy** to worry!

Turn what worries you over to God. He has **broad shoulders**. And then, free from the burden of worry, you just might **discover** how you can change things for the **better**.

*Dear God, let me leave my worries with You
as I listen to what you would have me do.*

No Worries

Find the reading's **bolded words** in the word search puzzle.

T	A	Q	Z	N	O	S	A	E	R	L	A	C	I	T	C	A	R	P	F	W	T
H	J	R	T	H	T	C	V	G	F	H	A	H	E	A	L	T	H	C	K	R	Q
G	Q	R	Y	S	E	V	R	E	W	O	P	U	M	P	J	T	E	L	E	W	C
U	G	L	R	Z	G	N	I	N	E	P	P	A	H	U	J	F	R	A	Y	D	K
O	N	X	N	E	A	Q	T	S	P	E	D	T	M	I	K	U	T	Q	K	Z	C
N	I	J	N	P	S	A	V	C	R	F	Y	G	T	Q	A	I	H	F	T	J	R
E	K	L	L	L	G	P	M	L	A	E	U	Z	U	I	N	I	I	W	L	P	C
L	N	W	I	M	O	H	O	W	S	B	D	Z	P	G	M	H	C	I	J	O	L
L	I	O	T	D	W	E	Y	N	M	P	T	L	S	F	O	E	Y	R	N	R	R
T	H	R	T	Y	W	K	C	L	D	I	I	X	U	F	C	G	F	T	J	N	E
J	T	R	L	N	Y	K	U	A	A	I	N	H	M	O	N	C	R	U	P	I	T
V	U	Y	E	Y	L	H	I	F	R	Q	N	D	S	V	H	O	M	Y	D	O	B
B	C	X	T	O	C	O	F	S	F	E	G	G	E	N	L	S	Z	S	Z	S	A
A	I	R	H	X	E	E	A	D	X	C	T	O	R	H	O	Q	D	V	F	U	V
P	X	H	I	Z	C	X	U	V	C	S	A	T	M	G	U	I	M	A	S	T	X
R	M	U	N	T	E	H	B	R	X	O	N	V	E	L	N	Z	T	D	O	R	M
J	R	Z	G	W	S	M	Z	T	E	Q	F	F	B	B	L	I	U	A	W	R	X
S	U	U	W	J	D	X	S	J	V	V	A	E	L	S	H	O	T	U	L	B	B
D	O	X	V	M	H	V	B	E	N	U	O	K	F	A	L	S	A	P	F	E	F
N	H	V	W	W	O	D	P	P	L	C	L	C	W	C	I	K	C	R	O	Z	R
A	E	H	D	L	G	U	F	C	V	P	W	Z	S	T	V	C	O	X	P	D	R
H	L	P	R	E	V	E	N	T	S	H	I	R	J	I	O	D	N	M	A	C	A
S	G	F	U	Z	D	P	W	Q	C	A	M	C	P	J	D	V	K	A	Y	D	J
D	N	N	K	F	A	Q	T	T	W	M	U	L	S	H	L	N	B	S	N	I	J
O	I	S	T	N	E	V	E	B	F	B	V	U	A	I	D	G	U	K	W	I	H
G	S	T	M	Z	X	S	N	A	U	J	N	U	G	O	D	B	I	L	O	L	F

CHAMPIONS

Some people have a lot to say about everybody else, don't they? Yet criticizing others is an easy habit to fall into. We notice that a friend, family member, or coworker isn't doing what we think they should be doing, and we unthinkingly weigh in with our opinions and criticisms.

More helpful, of course, would be a moment's thought. It's possible that they don't realize how their tone of voice comes across to us...what their behavior looks like in the eyes of others...when they need to ask for help in meeting their responsibilities...why their attempts at humor fall far short of the mark.

The world has enough critics, but it can always use champions. Champions are willing to think about what the other person might be going through...to take time to understand another person's perspective...to ask, "Can I help?"

Be a champion to someone today—it's critical for strong and fulfilling relationships.

Help me, dear God, encourage and support others with my words and actions.

Critical Words

Follow the clues by crossing off words in the grid. Some words might be crossed off by more than one clue. When you are finished, the remaining words form a saying, reading left to right.

✓ 1. Cross off all names of colors.
✓ 2. Cross off all words that rhyme with pan.
✓ 3. Cross off all foods and beverages.
✓ 4. Cross off all words containing two sets of double letters.
✓ 5. Cross off all words that are names of flowers or trees.
   6. Cross off all words that contain the word ant.

~~MILK~~	TWO	~~BUTTRESS~~	~~PLAN~~
~~THINGS~~	~~ROSE~~	ARE	~~GRANT~~
BAD	~~TEAL~~	~~CAN~~	FOR
~~COMMITTED~~	THE	~~PIE~~	~~PURPLE~~
HEART	~~OAK~~	RUNNING	~~PALM~~
UPSTAIRS	~~YELLOW~~	AND	RUNNING
~~PLEASANT~~	DOWN	~~AZURE~~	~~POMEGRANATE~~
~~SPAN~~	~~CORN~~	PEOPLE	~~ABBESS~~

Saying: _Two things are bad for the heart Running upstairs and running down people._

WHEN GOD SAYS "GO!"

Some decisions are scary to make, yet saying "yes" will open us to new, life-enhancing experiences. We're invited to learn more, do more, be more. Some beyond-our-wildest-dreams opportunities are there for us to enjoy to the fullest.

Are you afraid? Stop and pray. When God says Go, go for it!

Dear God, grant me the courage to go when You say Go!

Getting Going

You'll discover some encouraging words in this puzzle!

ACROSS
1. You might open a new one
4. Fury
8. President Coolidge, to friends
11. Respect
12. "Rock of __," traditional hymn
13. Cab
14. He fled from Sodom
15. Rascal
16. Goliath was one
17. Curdle
19. Mentor's student
20. Fib
21. Christmas figures
22. Native Alaskan
25. Down in the dumps
26. Lout
29. Affection
30. Elation
31. Wedding month
32. "Info forthcoming," for short
33. Prom rental, for short
34. Invigorating. Also descriptive of a lemon.
35. Yearn, with "for"
37. Letters in distress
38. Have faith in
40. Satisfied
44. Fervor
45. Asian garment
46. Johannesburg lander
47. Choir section
48. Accessible
49. Pipe type, for short
50. Seed bread
51. Floating ice
52. Fisherman's need

DOWN
1. Baby powder
2. Gone without permission, for short
3. Computer program test version
4. Hare
5. Come to an understanding
6. Wheel cog

DOWN CON'T

7 PST is three hours earlier than this
8 Wary
9 Shaft
10 Feel good about
13 Petty criminal
18 Unhappy
19 Little bit
21 Permission word
22 Keyboard key
23 Toss
24 Assess
25 Ball team, for short
27 Picnic visitor
28 Whimsical
30 Container
31 Prank
33 Explosive letters
34 Defining districts
36 Scandinavian capital
37 More angry
38 Former Russian ruler
39 Depend
40 Canaveral or Cod, for example
41 Athlete's network
42 Church section
43 Thoughtfulness
45 Cry

¹T	²A	³B	■	⁴R	⁵A	⁶B	⁷E	■	⁸C	⁹A	¹⁰L
¹¹A	W	E	■	¹²A	G	E	S	■	¹³T	A	X	I
¹⁴L	O	T	■	¹⁵B	R	A	T	■	¹⁶H	U	L	K
¹⁷C	L	A	¹⁸B	B	E	R	■	¹⁹J	U	T	E	E
■	■	■	²⁰L	I	E	■	²¹M	A	G	I	■	■
²²A	²³L	²⁴E	U	T	■	²⁵S	A	D	■	²⁶O	²⁷A	²⁸F
²⁹L	O	V	E	■	³⁰J	O	Y	■	³¹J	U	N	E
³²T	B	A	■	³³T	U	X	■	³⁴Z	E	S	T	Y
■	■	³⁵L	³⁶O	N	G	■	³⁷S	O	S	■	■	■
³⁸T	³⁹R	U	S	T	■	⁴⁰C	O	N	T	⁴¹E	⁴²N	⁴³T
⁴⁴Z	E	A	L	■	⁴⁵S	A	R	I	■	⁴⁶S	A	A
⁴⁷A	L	T	O	■	⁴⁸O	P	E	N	■	⁴⁹P	V	C
⁵⁰R	Y	E	■	⁵¹B	E	R	G	■	⁵²N	E	T

17

CHANGE IN SEASON

There's no getting away from change! The seasons change, each with its own beauty and adventure, surprises and challenges. That's similar to the seasons of life, too. Each one holds opportunities and limitations, gains and losses, joy and mystery.

Change is natural, but it often throws us in unfamiliar territory. Sometimes we just don't want to go there! It invites us to explore new ideas, questions, and perspectives, and that makes us feel uncertain and afraid. It pushes us to find new ways of doing things, yet we'd rather keep on doing what we've always been doing. That's natural, too.

It takes a brave heart to take on change. You can do it. The season you're in right now holds opportunities that you could never have known before. You possess insights that come only with years of living and know-how that reflect tried-and-true, hands-on experience. Highlight these things. Take pride in them. They are all part of you, with still more to come.

Change isn't always easy, but remember this: God never changes. His love is the same yesterday, today, and forever!

Dear God, help me see the blessings
You have granted every season of life.

Transformations

Change the first word into the second word of each pair by replacing only one letter at a time. Do not scramble letter order; use only common English words, and no capitalized words.

Example:

>   LOSE
>   lone
>   line
>   fine
>   FIND

1. TINY

   _____
   _____
   _____
   _____
   _____

   VAST

2. POOR

   _____
   _____
   _____
   _____
   _____

   RICH

3. LESS

   _____
   _____
   _____
   _____
   _____

   MORE

4. MEAN

   _____
   _____
   _____
   _____
   _____

   KIND

5. HOLD

   _____
   _____
   _____
   _____
   _____

   GIVE

IT'S ABOUT TIME

What eats up big chunks of time? For many of us, it's not the big, important activities of the day, but small, insignificant tasks and minor, pesky distractions. If we were to keep track of how many hours we spend each day doing things that have little or nothing to do with what we had planned to do, we would be surprised!

If you wonder where your time is going, keep track of your activities for a few days or a week. Discover where you are spending valuable hours doing things that aren't necessary, mean little to you, and fail to match your goals and objectives. Only you can judge, because only you know what matters most to you and what brings you joy and satisfaction.

Give yourself the gift of time. Minimize distractions, delegate where you can, and let go of activities that no longer fit your needs. Open up some time for *you*.

Dear God, show me how to use my time wisely, joyfully, and productively.

Timely Matters

All the answers in this puzzle are related to time.

ACROSS
3 Timeless
5 "One day is with the Lord as a thousand __..." (2 Peter 3:8)
9 "Teach us to __ our days" (Psa. 90:12)
11 "Time is __," says the starter
13 "Time is __," says the boss
16 __ Saving Time
17 "Time __," says the harried one
18 Calendar heading

DOWN

1. "In __ time," says the procrastinator
2. "A time of war, a time of __" (Eccl. 3:8)
4. "Time and __ wait for no man"
6. "It's __ time!" sighs the impatient one
7. "A time to every __ under the heaven" (Eccl. 3:1)
8. "Time and __ happeneth to them all" (Eccl. 9:11)
10. "The Lord will deliver him in time of __" (Psa. 41:1)
12. "Time heals all __"
14. "Time is too __," says the busy one
15. Time keeper

EASY DOESN'T DO IT

Who doesn't like it when things come easy? And they certainly do whenever we take the easy way out. The easy way of forming an opinion or reaching a conclusion is this: take what most other people are saying and make it your own. Make decisions based on a fleeting impression...a moment's thought...an old, but familiar, saying.

Things come easy when we excuse ourselves from taking on our God-given responsibilities...from finding ways to lessen the burdens of others...from trying to do better today than we did yesterday. Sure, we'd escape many of life's challenges and struggles, but we'd also miss life's joys.

Think about the times you have felt most alive, most productive, most satisfied. Remember when you felt proud of yourself and glad that you did what you did. In all likelihood, you were engaged in doing something meaningful and purposeful. You had taken the initiative to put yourself out there, overcome what might have stood in your way, and continue even if things weren't particularly easy.

God is there to strengthen you, especially when the going isn't easy. "I will strengthen you and help you" is His promise to you (Isaiah 41:10 niv).

Dear God, give me the strength I need
to continue when things aren't easy for me.

Missions Accomplished

Many Bible stories highlight what happens when God-trusting men and women choose "difficult" over "easy." Match the name in the first column with the event in the second column.

1. David — D. Took on a hardened warrior, though a youth and armed only with a stone.

2. Abraham — H. Uprooted his household and set out for a land promised to him by God.

3. Deborah — A. Led an army against the fearsome Canaanites and defeated them.

4. Paul — F. Endured imprisonment and floggings, yet continued to preach the Gospel message.

5. Ananias — I. Approached a known persecutor of the early church because God told him to do so.

6. Esther — J. Risked her life to save her people from a genocidal plot.

7. Moses — B. Demanded that Pharaoh let God's people leave Egypt.

8. Joseph — G. Married his pregnant fiancée because God told him in a dream that she would give birth to Jesus.

9. John — C. Lived in the desert and preached repentance to the people.

10. Jonah — E. Sent by God to preach repentance to the Ninevites, even though he was reluctant to do so.

Big Puzzler

People and places of the Bible are in this crossword puzzle!

ACROSS

1. Trims
6. Go quickly
10. Snow skidder
14. "Come unto me, all ye that... are heavy __" (Matt. 11:28)
15. Patmos, for example
16. Eastern church altar area
17. Dramatic production song
18. Decorative needle case
19. Deliver us from __
20. Some ark pairs
22. Henhouse gatherings
24. Old Testament priest
25. Colder
27. Cozy and comfortable
29. Old Testament patriarch
32. Couple
33. Shout of disapproval
34. Sinai leader
37. Eve's Husband
41. Writer Bombeck
43. Child
44. Infant in Paris
45. Ogle
46. Bethlehem Baby
48. Body builder's pride, for short
49. Self
51. Old Testament judge
54. Son of 29 Across
56. Prison
57. School org.
58. Speak with trilled "r"
60. Sawmill's product
64. "__ of milk and honey"
66. You have two when you tie your shoe
68. Gaelic name meaning white or fair
69. Bread spread
70. In addition
71. Monies
72. Old Testament King Hiram's city
73. "Spirit of the Lord shall __ upon him" (Isa. 11:2)
74. Destroy

DOWN

1. Messy one
2. Neck part
3. Thought
4. Queen Esther's realm
5. Kidnap
6. What 46 Across did on Calvary
7. Autumn flower
8. Bogus coin
9. Elevations
10. Joppa to Jerusalem dir.
11. Barrier
12. Poet Dickinson
13. Painter of melting clocks
21. "Anna and the King of __"
23. "They that __ in tears shall reap in joy" (Psa. 126:5)
26. Express feelings
28. Utah biking region
29. Son of 37 Across
30. "He himself __ our sins" (1 Peter 2:24 NIV)
31. Paul's place of house arrest
35. Distress call
36. Musical practice piece

DOWN Con't

38 Letter opener
39 "We cry, ___, Father" (Romans 8:15)
40 Netting
42 Region
46 Given to joking
47 "Buy the truth, and ___ it not" (Pro. 23:23)
50 Chatter
52 Cliffs
53 Metallic element
54 31 Down location
55 More reasonable
56 Calvary sight
57 Judas' plan, for example
59 a character's part, as for 17 across
61 ___ fide
62 Ceases
63 Impulsive
65 Fawn's mom
67 Urn

TRUE LOVE

Many of us grew up **hearing stories** and **watching movies** about valiant princes and **beautiful** princesses. They all lived **happily** ever after! We **longed** for the day when that **special** someone would come into **our lives** and love us **faithfully** and **exclusively** forever. That's **what** we knew about love!

As we **mature**, however, we **realize** that there are many **kinds of** love. **Romantic** love, **of course**...but also love **between** parent and child...love for **our friends**...love among those **belonging** to the same **congregation**...love of **country**...love of **life itself**. The word "love" is **packed** with meaning, **emotion**, and **positive images**.

Yet more meanings **unfold** with the **passing years**. Your love **grows** and **deepens**. Each day, **express** your love by showing love to the **people** with whom you **share** your life, and **thank them** for all the ways they show their love to you. Love is a **gift**, an **adventure**. Never shut **yourself** away from the **blessing** of loving and being loved, because "**God is love**" (1 John 4:8).

*Dear God, thank You for loving me,
and show me how to love others faithfully and unselfishly.*

God Is Love

Find the reading's **bolded words** in the word search puzzle.

```
Y E N O U R F R I E N D S I E I H F D X F A
C M X U D N V B L E S S I N G K U D O F D H
A O A E X C L U S I V E L Y U V L T W V E U
Q T T F Y Q Y J X C E O T J R O P V E A D G
C I B C B E T W E E N C F V F K Q N R W M H
G O G O D I S L O V E L C N O V T I Q R A K
P N R E V P X U V G E B U U X U N H L P S F
G M F V G L O G L S G I F T R G S D P F V O
P R P N X E E N T R F J R E S R G I Y I U P
W R O L O N G I F G P L C T A I L I Y R A C
U S L W T T E Q F I O F O E F Y M U L C F I
H C H T S F D B E N P R Y W I Z X I K V F T
U J S A I Q L X G G I G L A U S V E G C V N
Y D P L R V H E R E N E C U E E D D L O A A
J A E G T E D Q S I S M Z G S B B E U N A M
S M C O B I W U S R K L A P M O E E F G H O
Y B I F K T G S U S K M B K O R L P I R Y R
L K A G A G A O O C I P T I J O O E T E O C
L C L S D P C V A E K E T N F J N N U G U U
U S D E Y F V M V E Y O W D I E G S A A R E
F S H M O T Q I Z R O P U S A O I B E T S R
H E Y L H G T I T Q T L O O L N N M B I E U
T R P V L I L N R A P E Q F Z R G V X O L T
I P H O S A U K H Y R I N H G O W R A N F A
A X D O E O H W A T C H I N G M O V I E S M
F E P R C X Z D T H A N K T H E M G U B O J
```

WORTH REPEATING

Most of the time, we rely on familiar habits and learned behavior to see us through our interactions with others and daily responsibilities. It's possible, however, that only some of our words and actions work to our good and the good of others. Only some give us the results we really want.

Every evening for the next several days, go over what happened during the day. Jot down what worked and what could have been better. Note the things you said and did that are worth repeating day in and day out...and also the things you said and did that did not work for the positive.

What will you do differently tomorrow? How can you change what doesn't work into what does work, and is truly worth repeating the next day and the next and the next?

Show me, dear God, how to change my behavior so my words and actions bless my life and the lives of the people I meet.

Rhyme Time

Each clue can be answered with two rhyming words. All refer to a well-known Bible figure, and the spaces show how many letters are in the answer. Example:

Adam's son's great canines = **CAIN'S DANES**

1. First woman's wheat bundles
__ __ __'__ __ __ __ __ __

2. Gospel writer's English noblemen
__ __ __ __'__ __ __ __ __ __

3. Ark builder's feathery scarves
__ __ __ __'__ __ __ __ __

4. Naomi's faithful daughter-in-law's small enclosures
__ __ __ __'__ __ __ __ __ __ __

5. Moses' brother's long-legged wading birds
__ __ __ __ __'__ __ __ __ __ __ __

6. Gospel writer's green spaces
__ __ __ __ __'__ __ __ __ __ __

7. Epistle writer's fairground shelters
__ __ __ __ __'__ __ __ __ __ __ __

8. The Baptizer's young deer
__ __ __ __'__ __ __ __ __ __

9. Sodom fleer's little children
__ __ __'__ __ __ __ __

10. Israel's first king's shopping arcades
__ __ __ __'__ __ __ __ __ __

FAMILY MATTERS

The perfect family doesn't exist today, and didn't in Bible times, either. Yet then as now, there were men and women, teens and children—family members—who loved, not because those around them were always lovable, but because they chose to love. Their devotion to one another grew as a natural fruit of their dedication to God and their commitment to following His will in all their relationships.

Remember that God's Son, Jesus, was born into a family. He grew up in the city of Nazareth surrounded by relatives, friends, and neighbors, which means He heard His share of words that should not have been said. But also words of caring, love, tenderness, and encouragement. Acts of helpfulness, kindness, and forgiveness.

Your natural family and your spiritual family are made up of imperfect individuals, each with strengths and weaknesses. Through your words and actions, you can guide and inspire, help and encourage. You can be the one who knows—and shows—what being family is all about.

Dear God, let me be the one who brings
the blessings of encouragement, respect, kindness,
and peace to my family in whatever way I can.

All in the Family

Get acquainted with these Bible families! Match the description in the first column with the family member in the second column.

1. Jesus often visited the Bethany home of Mary and Martha and their brother.
2. This beloved son of King David connived to take his father's throne.
3. Jesus healed this disciple's mother-in-law's fever.
4. In the very first family, this son murdered his brother, Abel.
5. Their jealousy led his eleven brothers to sell him into slavery.
6. Leaving their father Zebedee's fishing business, James and his brother went to follow Jesus.
7. King David's son with Bathsheba was renowned for his wisdom and wealth.
8. This missionary followed his mother Eunice and grandmother Lois in the faith.
9. Abraham's wife bore a son, Isaac, late in life.
10. This faithful daughter-in-law left her own land to go with her widowed mother-in-law, Naomi.
11. His brother Aaron spoke for him in front of Pharaoh of Egypt.
12. He fathered 12 sons and one daughter by Leah, Rachel, and their maidservants.

A. Peter
B. John
C. Ruth
D. Solomon
E. Sarah
F. Cain
G. Moses
H. Joseph
I. Timothy
J. Lazarus
K. Jacob
L. Absalom

YOU CAN BANK ON IT

Asked to name the most-mentioned topics in the Bible, you might think of God...Jesus...heaven...faith. What might not come to mind is the subject of money. Yet there are over 2,000 references to money, wealth, and possessions throughout Scripture!

Our view of money reflects our relationship with God and those around us. If we think security lies in how much money we have, contentment depends on how much stuff we possess, and self-worth can be counted in dollars, then we have a big problem. Money can't fill even one of those needs!

Put God first by looking to Him for guidance concerning the money He has put under your management. Spend, save, and share what you have in ways that meet your needs and the needs of others, all without letting money become your life's focus. Discover your true wealth in becoming closer to Him in faith, relying on Him for your ultimate security, and looking to Him for your inner peace and well-being. For God promises, "Seek first his kingdom and his righteousness, and all these things will be given to you as well" (Matthew 6:33 niv).

Help me, dear God, develop a healthy relationship to money so I will be led to use it as You intend me to use it.

Funny Money

See if you know the answer to these money questions!

1. According to records, who guarded the first U.S. Mint in Philadelphia?
   a. A watchdog
   b. Two soldiers
   c. It wasn't guarded

2. If you stack 48 pennies, how high would your stack be?
   a. 1 inch
   b. 2 inches
   c. 3 inches

3. About how much was the price of a gallon of gas in 1950?
   a. 10 cents
   b. 20 cents
   c. 30 cents

4. The first non-mythical person to appear on a regular-issue U.S. coin was President Lincoln in 1909. Who was the first non-mythical woman to appear?
   a. Martha Washington
   b. Susan B. Anthony
   c. Queen Isabella of Spain

5. What dollar denomination is a Benjamin?
   a. $50
   b. $100
   c. $500

6. Approximately how much does the average American spend on fast food annually?
   a. $1,000
   b. $3,000
   c. $5,000

7. What percent of income is a literal tithe?
   a. 5%
   b. 10%
   c. 15%

8. During which war did the United States first start printing bills?
   a. Revolutionary War
   b. Spanish-American War
   c. Civil War

9. How much does it cost to produce a nickel?
   a. Less than it costs to produce a dime
   b. More than it costs to produce a dime
   c. About the same as it costs to produce a dime

10. About how long does a dollar bill last in circulation?
    a. Less than 6 years
    b. More than 10 years
    c. Only one year

GOD KNOWS

Suddenly things change...there is sickness, hardship, loss. How desperately we want to fix things, to put them back to where they were! Yet not one of us has that kind of power. But we possess the power of prayer.

Use your prayer-power to ask God to change things, and at the same time, acknowledge His higher wisdom and accept His divine purpose.

Dear God, teach me to trust that with you,
my cares are in good hands.

Prayer Power

Many of the words in this puzzle are related to prayer.

ACROSS

1 Truth
5 Prep school (Abbr.)
9 Uninvolved
11 "Thy will be ___"
12 Child-bearer
13 Avant-garde art movement
14 Joppa to Jerusalem dir.
15 Computer memory unit
17 Commandments number
18 Tan colors
20 How Solomon judged
22 Sect.
23 Providence locale (Abbr.)
24 Early patriot's descendent, perhaps
27 "Deliver us from ___"
29 "Make a joyful ___ unto the Lord" (Psa. 100:1)
31 4-wheeler
32 "Ask, and it shall be ___ you" (Matt. 7:7)
33 Org.
34 "___ us not into temptation"

DOWN

1. Renown
2. "__! and Did My Savior Bleed?" hymn title
3. "Thy kingdom __"
4. Cat
5. Total
6. Raccoon-like animal
7. South American mountain range
8. College head
10. "Our __," prayer opening
16. Making bundles of hay
18. Topeka locale (Abbr.)
19. Paducah locale (Abbr.)
20. Leah and Rachel to Jacob
21. Crawling vines
22. __ vu
24. Swimming pool jump
25. Not ashore
26. "A time to __, and a time to sew" (Eccl. 3:7)
28. Hosp. staffer
30. "Thou anointest my head with __" (Psa. 23:5)

COMING UP ROSES

"Some people complain because God put thorns among roses," the saying goes, "while others thank Him for putting roses among thorns." Yes, some of us focus on what's wrong with the world, and there's always *something wrong*. Some of us, however, have made the decision to highlight what's right with the world, and there's always *something right!*

Imagine two people, both facing the same challenge. One sits and moans, telling anyone who will listen how put upon, how unfortunate, he is. The other gets up and does whatever is possible to improve his situation. One throws her hands in the air...the other puts her hands to work. One stares at the thorns and does nothing...the other smells the roses and gives thanks.

Today, treat yourself to a dozen roses. Name 12 things you're glad about and take pleasure in the beauty of a thankful heart.

Thank You, dear God, for the 12 special blessings I have in my heart right now.

Flower Show

Unscramble the letters for a list of favorite flowers. Then unscramble the letters in parenthesis for another colorful flower, and you'll have a full bouquet!

1. A A T N O N R C I

   _ _ _ _ _ _ (_) _ _

2. L F D F D O A I

   _ (_) _ _ _ _ _ _

3. S O G L U I D L A

   _ _ _ (_) _ _ _ _ _

4. P A A G R O D N S N

   (_) _ _ _ _ _ _ _ _ _

5. S A N Y P

   _ _ _ (_) _

6. Z L E A A A

   _ _ _ _ (_) _

7. H D I A A L

   _ _ _ _ (_) _

   Answer: _ _ _ _ _ _ _

UNDER COVER

At the meeting, she paid attention to the facilitator, asked questions, and participated in the discussion. During the break, she chatted amicably with friends and introduced herself to newcomers. Only a few in the room knew that she was undergoing monthly medical treatments that left her weak and sick for days.

Appearances can be deceiving. Most of the time, we have no idea what the person sitting next to us has gone through or is going through...what the man or woman standing in the checkout line is up against...what tough realities the stranger passing us on the sidewalk has faced in his life. Because they look just like us, and we, too, have our share of stories to tell.

Your patience and kindness, tolerance and gentleness can come as a ray of sunshine in someone's day. Your smile can let someone know she's not alone...he's not forgotten...and you care.

Dear God, open my heart to the needs of others.

Hidden Words

These sentences aren't what they appear to be! In each sentence, find as many of the hidden words listed below.

Example: TAP   EARS   RAN   TOME

It appears st**ra**nge **to me**.

SWORD	FAST	RYE	LIES
RED	RISE	MAR	VENUE
HOOT	TAN	WERE	ANT
SHE	DREW	AWL	ACT
STOVE	WED	HANG	DREAD
ARM	INK	RUE	SENT
MINT	OUT	VENT	QUEST
LESSEN	PAT	NEIGH	WORD
EVEN	ROUGH	TORN	

1. Miles sensed that Mary's words were true.

2. Charlie says he met another neighbor.

3. Who's to venture down this path?

4. Are we driving east or north, or are we really lost?

5. Who other than Gary owns a farm?

6. I'm in the middle of a startling presentation, can't you tell?

7. His dad read an adventure story every evening.

8. No question, her facts surprised us.

9. I'm thinking Andrew crawled through the avenue.

WAY MORE

Picture a harvester approaching a field. But instead of bringing a basket for the yield, he shows up with a teacup! Clearly, he doesn't think he'll gather much. Even if he finds an abundance, he isn't prepared to take it home.

If you go to God with small expectations, you're like the teacup-bearing harvester. Your God is a God of huge harvests! He loves to give, and give more besides. With God, spread your arms wide open!

Dear God, thank You for Your generosity to me.

Abundance Abounds

Here's a puzzle designed around the theme of abundance.

ACROSS

1 Significant
3 Outstanding; awesome
9 Big-hearted
11 Hope for
12 Limitless
14 Crop
16 Riches
17 Bestow
20 __-of-the-crop
21 "He which soweth bountifully shall __ also bountifully" (2 Corinthians 9:6)
22 Big
23 Satisfied
25 Ask God
27 Awe-struck
28 Gives aid to
29 Present

DOWN

2 "My cup runneth __" (Psa. 23:5)
4 Surpass
5 Lush; abundant
6 "Ask what I shall __ thee" (1 Kings 3:5)
7 Ample
8 Advantages
10 Bring to
11 Continual
13 "There shall be __ of blessing" (Eze. 34:26)
15 Choicest
17 Unearned mercy
18 Show favor to
19 Lots
24 Most pleasant
26 Reap

41

VOCABULARY LESSON

What have you told yourself lately? Do you use the same words and phrases that you would say to someone you love? If not, give yourself a vocabulary lesson. Throw out demeaning, derisive, and degrading expressions—these do nothing but lure you into believing what you keep hearing in your mind.

Now for some strong, healthy, and productive replacements. How about words along the lines of good, super, excellent? Phrases such as "I learned something here" and "I'll do better next time" do far more to help you than any self-deprecating thought-lashings. Words of encouragement and self-forgiveness go a long way toward freeing you from feelings of shame and inferiority.

Words can tear you down or build you up...push you backward or pull you forward...cause you pain or bring you joy. They can dampen your life with low expectations or color your life with endless possibilities. They can make you frown or make you smile...cry or laugh... despair or hope. The words you say to yourself—the words you use, repeat, and believe—matter.

Dear God, let me speak to myself as to someone You dearly love—because You do.

Good Words

Pick the definition that best fits the "good word" provided.

1. EFFERVESCENT
a. Kind
b. Lively
c. Nice

2. INTREPID
a. Courageous
b. Gentle
c. Agreeable

3. ESTEEMED
a. Essential
b. Honored
c. Nurturing

4. ETHICAL
a. Enthusiastic
b. Secure
c. Principled

5. COMMENDABLE
a. Worthy
b. Intelligent
c. Poised

6. PROLIFIC
a. Productive
b. Friendly
c. Clean

7. EMPATHETIC
a. Powerful
b. Zealous
c. Understanding

8. HUMANITARIAN
a. Compassionate
b. Fun
c. Popular

9. CONTEMPLATIVE
a. Contented
b. Reflective
c. Graceful

10. MUNIFICENT
a. Distinguished
b. Generous
c. Lucid

11. INTUITIVE
a. Fortunate
b. Celebrated
c. Perceptive

12. PHENOMENAL
a. Extraordinary
b. Unwavering
c. Harmonious

BE HAPPY

Most of us could name what we think would make us happy. A fatter paycheck, a dream vacation, a new home might be high on the list. How about the freedom to do whatever we want? Certainly any one of these things might bring us temporary happiness. But long-lasting happiness lies where we might not expect to find it.

Happiness that lasts lies not in doing what you want all the time, but in doing what God asks you to do...not in getting more, but in being content with what you have right now...not in gratifying yourself, but in sharing with others, putting yourself out for others, and delighting others with gentle words and thoughtful gestures...in helping others, even when it's inconvenient to do so. No one can take away this kind of happiness, because it isn't outside of you. It's in you. It's an integral part of you.

The way to happiness is counter-intuitive, isn't it? But that's often the way it is with things that really matter.

Dear God, give me the courage
to drop my old ideas and do the things that
You know will bring true and lasting happiness.

Happy Discoveries

Put the answer to Clue 1 in box 1. Scramble the letters and drop one letter to answer Clue 2. Write the word in box 2 and the dropped letter in the left-hand box. Scramble the letters and drop one letter to answer Clue 3. Write the word in box 3 and the dropped letter in the right-hand box. Complete each row the same way, starting with a new word. When you're finished, you'll discover two new words reading vertically on both sides of the puzzle. The first line is already done for you.

1. Bed needs
2. Not those
3. KJV pronoun
4. Small field rodent
5. A few
6. Fruct- or gluc- ending
7. Ankle ailment, maybe
8. Couples
9. Box
10. Citrus
11. Yard burrower
12. One of the Three Stooges
13. Weepy
14. Price
15. Pothole filler

S	1. *sheets*	2. *these*	3. *thee*	S
	4.	5.	6.	
	7.	8.	9.	
	10.	11.	12.	
	13.	14.	15.	

THIS IS THE DAY

Contentment doesn't mean we have to stop dreaming or desire and never want anything more than what we have now. That would be resignation! No, contentment is active, involved, hopeful, and motivated...but at the same time, pleased with the present.

Where you are right now is your stepping stone to the future. Claim it...use it...take pleasure in it...use it! Delve into the moment so you can experience it fully and wring from it any learning, lesson, or opportunity it may provide to make tomorrow even better, richer, more fulfilling, more exciting. Delight in the present, because it's the most precious resource you possess.

True contentment is active and busy with what is at hand. "This is the day which the Lord hath made; we will rejoice and be glad in it" (Psalm 118:24).

Dear God, I want to experience contentment today as I reach toward tomorrow.

Active Contentment

Many words are spelled the same, but have different meanings, and sometimes different pronunciations. In each sentence below, replace the bolded words with one word. Example:

Her manager was **satisfied** with the **substance** of her report.
Answer: **content**

1. It was a **pleasant** day until he got a **ticket** for speeding.
   Answer: _____

2. He's the **only one** who had to repair the **bottom** of his shoe.
   Answer: _____

3. She didn't feel **fit** when she looked into the **mineshaft**, so the event didn't go **satisfactorily**.
   Answer: _____

4. "It's only **just**," she said as we walked around the arts and crafts **show**.
   Answer: _____

5. I saw her **curtsy** on the **front** of the ship.
   Answer: _____

6. Do you have a **clue** about the group that he **facilitated**?
   Answer: _____

7. Some of the coffee I **milled** spilled all over the **lawn**.
   Answer: _____

8. It was on the **edge** of her tongue to say we should leave a more generous **gratuity**.
   Answer: _____

9. Who wants to **abandon** the group in the Mohave **sands**?
   Answer: _____

10. Despite the cold **breeze**, I continued to **meander** around the garden and **coil** the hose.
    Answer: _____

11. He **stood up** from his chair and gave her a red **flower**.
    Answer: _____

12. No one knew she had **gobbled** down her lunch and had **disappeared** through the **latched** door.
    Answer: _____

13. There was a **conflict** over who would stand in the first **line**.
    Answer: _____

14. The **water bird** would have to **bend down** to get under the bridge.
    Answer: _____

15. The **council** members all sat at a **table** made with a **plank** and two sawhorses.
    Answer: _____

16. We'll be in a real **fix** if there's a traffic **slowdown** between here and there.
    Answer: _____

17. Let's **get back to** looking at her **application**.
    Answer: _____

ALL THERE

"Be there—or be square!" The phrase rarely fails to bring a chuckle. More important than any place we might go, however, is that we're there not just in body, but in heart and mind. We're present to the moment and taking in the whole experience, using our time, wherever we are, to the fullest.

Aware...seeing...hearing...observing...participating...being there brings a whole new dimension to even the most routine, ordinary day. This moment is something you can never replace, renew, or retrieve. Be there!

Thank You, dear God, for the precious moments
You have given to me this day.

Attention!

Many clues in this puzzle are designed to get your attention!

ACROSS

1 Hand holder
4 Couple
5 Some time back
6 Time piece
9 Loch __ monster
13 Vase
14 Affirmative
15 High schooler
17 Desire
18 "Three persons, __ God"
20 Promise
21 "Our Father who __ in heaven"

DOWN

1. Esther's month
2. Floor covering
3. Night light
6. Shelter
7. Miner's goal
8. French number
10. View
11. Notice
12. Downhearted
16. Shining star
17. Salamander
19. Neither's partner

🍀 NUMBER ONE

In athletic competitions, each contestant wants to win the gold medal. Yet only one person can, and it's not easy to rank number one when you're surrounded by many others who want first place for themselves. You have to fend off all comers. Through years of building skill, strength, and endurance, you aim to be the one who takes home the trophy.

In life, there's no winner-take-all, and we have no need to out-perform everyone around us. That isn't the purpose of life. There's still competition, however—competition with ourselves. Rather than rest on our laurels—those past successes, awards, and recognitions—we use them as springboards to even greater triumphs today. Maybe we won't achieve again in exactly the same way, or go at a goal with the same force, vigor, and energy as we did earlier in life, or even get the kind of recognition we once did. But we will continue to explore new ideas and try new skills. We were able to grow, and there's no reason why we should stop growing now.

Look back and count up your successes. You tried to do it, and you did it. You set your sights on something, and you won it. How do you choose to challenge yourself today?

Dear God, let me believe that I can do it.

Games We Play

Challenge yourself to pick the right answer for these sports-related questions!

1. In which sport would you hear the terms "stalefish" and "mule kick" used?
   a. Skiing
   b. Swimming
   c. Snowboarding

2. Where was Super Bowl I played?
   a. Los Angeles, California
   b. Atlanta, Georgia
   c. Green Bay, Wisconsin

3. What is the maximum amount of time a golfer can look for a lost ball?
   a. 2 minutes
   b. 3 minutes
   c. 5 minutes

4. In 1994, why was there no baseball World Series?
   a. Players were on strike
   b. Coaches were on strike
   c. Hot dog vendors were on strike

5. Which sport did George Washington play with his troops?
   a. Kickball
   b. Soccer
   c. Cricket

6. When was the Indianapolis Motor Speedway for car racing built?
   a. 1909
   b. 1929
   c. 1939

7. In the modern Olympic games, when were women first admitted as athletes?
   a. 1886
   b. 1900
   c. 1904

8. When was the first Wimbledon tennis tournament held?
   a. 1802
   b. 1877
   c. 1905

9. Which country dominates Olympics basketball?
   a. USA
   b. Brazil
   c. Sweden

10. In which sport are wickets used?
    a. Soccer
    b. Darts
    c. Cricket

Big Puzzler

This puzzle is full of sports-related words!

ACROSS

1 Nebraska city
6 Camper's bed
9 Internist's org. (Abbr.)
12 Intense light beam
13 Cheerleader's cry
14 Caustic substance
15 Moral principles
16 Sin
17 Fall mo. (Abbr.)
18 Present
20 Plant reproductive structure
22 Diamond figure
25 More subtly ridiculing
26 Put together
27 Tennis need
29 Stir
31 Billiards player's need
32 First letter of the Arabic alphabet
36 Remain loyal (2 wds.)
39 Whiz
40 Black belt wearer's study
43 Scratched
45 Horse sound
46 Fan sound
47 Steamer's initials
48 Climate watchdog group (Abbr.)
50 Blood carriers
54 Caviar
55 Team sports figure, for short
56 Listlessness
57 Hosp. staffer
58 What the benched player did
59 Raves partner

DOWN

1 Stadium cry
2 Exerciser's need, perhaps
3 Tree type
4 Robbery
5 Bow and arrow user
6 Sailing team
7 Canoe propeller
8 King's chair
9 Aurally discernable
10 Two-wheeler, for short
11 Christ's disciple
19 Prophet of ancient times
21 Brief autobiographical sketch
22 Cave flyer

DOWN CON'T

23 Hoopla
24 Football goals (Abbr.)
25 Draw
28 What a cow chews
30 Thick carpet
33 Rule
34 Winter hazard
35 Nourished
37 Not us
38 "__ Twist," Dickens title
40 Projecting ridge
41 Fable writer
42 "He is __!" Easter proclamation
44 Athletic field
46 Blow
49 Legume
51 Hotel
52 Almond, e.g.
53 Sibling, for short

SUNNY DAYS

What's the first thought that crosses your mind the moment you wake up? Chances are that whatever you say to yourself in those few seconds will set the tone for the entire day ahead of you.

If words and feelings of fear, dread, or hopelessness greet you in the morning, refuse to let them tag along with you as you go about your day. All they will do is drag you down and make any difficulties seem worse than they really are. Negative thoughts also keep you from fully appreciating your present blessings and enjoying the truly good things all around you.

Replace negative thoughts with positive ones, like "I'm going to feel good today"…"I will make sure I compliment someone today"… "I'm going to do my best and leave the rest to God." Need a daily reminder? Put a short, positive, and meaningful note next to your alarm clock or on your bathroom mirror. Repeat it to yourself when you wake up, and make up your mind to be happy.

There are many things you can't control, but you can control your frame of mind. Begin with a sunny attitude, and it will light your way all day long.

Dear God, fill my mind with positive thoughts
that I can take with me throughout the day.

Weather Forecast

Match the biblical weather event with the person or place involved.

1. There was a storm on the Sea of Galilee...

2. The sun turned dark...

3. It rained 40 days and nights...

4. The sun stood still...

5. A windstorm brought tongues of fire...

6. A windstorm brought a plague of locusts...

7. A great wind tore mountains and shattered rocks...

8. An earthquake dislodged a great stone...

9. Hot sun and wind withered a shady plant...

10. Spiritual dryness robs the soul of nourishment...

a. ...and the Holy Spirit descended upon the disciples.

b. ...but Noah and his family were safe in the ark.

c. ...but Pharaoh would not let the children of Israel leave Egypt.

d. ...but the Lord was not in it, but in a still, small voice.

e. ...and Jonah was angry with God because of his discomfort.

f. ...and the disciples saw Jesus walk on water.

g. ...and women found not Jesus, but an empty tomb.

h. ...and Jesus died.

I. ...but God provides comfort and sustenance to the hungry.

j. ...and the children of Israel won the battle against their enemies.

HEAD-ON PROBLEM SOLVING

Problems aren't fun. When they come our way, we naturally want to run and hide, hoping they'll just go someplace else and leave us alone. Yet the best thing we can do is come right out and meet them head-on. The sooner, the better!

When we give our full attention to a problem that's confronting us, we're able not only to determine what it is, but also what it is not. Clear-eyed seeing leaves no room for imagination to run away with us and send us into panic mode. Fact-based thinking allows us to figure out how to meet and resolve the issue at hand. Often a huge problem can be broken down into small, fixable pieces. Or perhaps we can find others who can help or advise us, or there's a place we can go to get the resources we need. Or maybe the problem is going to be with us for a while, and we can discover how to cope effectively with the challenge.

All problems, even the toughest problems you face, have one good thing in common. Each is an invitation to grow more...pray more...and lean more on God, the source of your strength.

Give me the courage, dear God, to meet my problems head-on.

Solutions

Unscramble each solution-oriented word, and when you are finished, unscramble the letters in parenthesis for another important point!

1. K H N I T   L L R Y E C A

_ _ _ _ _   _ _ _(_)_ _ _

2. E S E R A R H C

(_)_ _ _ _ _ _ _ _

3. O T I C J V B I T Y E

_ _ _ _ _ _ _ _ _ _(_)

4. R S N T E N D C I M E

_ _ _ _(_)_ _ _ _ _ _

5. R O T O   U S E C A

(_)_ _ _   _ _ _ _ _ _

6. N N N L G P A I

(_)_ _ _ _ _ _ _ _

Solution: _ _ _ _ _ _

LAUGHTER

"If you can laugh at yourself," someone once quipped, "you'll always have something to laugh at!"

God-blessed humor is kindly and well-intentioned, friendly and lighthearted. It defuses tension, lifts moods, and encourages others to see the bright side. Most of all, it can step away from itself, look back, and laugh.

Dear God, fill my life with loving, kindly, and joyful laugher.

Very Funny!

Each answer in this puzzle relates to the theme of laughter.

ACROSS

- 2 "In a good __"
- 6 Radiant
- 8 Laughter
- 10 Circus comic
- 11 Gain pleasure from
- 16 Make glad (2 words0
- 17 "Happy as a __"
- 18 "On cloud __"
- 19 Entertain
- 21 Jubilant
- 22 Face of laughter
- 24 Joke
- 26 Smile maker
- 27 "Look on the __ side"
- 28 Good disposition
- 29 "Happy as a __ bug"

DOWN

- 1 Cleverly funny
- 3 Glee
- 4 "__ on air"
- 5 "__ pink"
- 7 "A __ heart hath a continual feast" (Prov. 15:15)
- 9 "On top of the __"

DOWN Con't

10 Quiet laughter
12 Great pleasure
13 Take part in recreation
14 "In seventh __"
15 Smile broadly
17 Some TV shows
20 Positive
23 Paradise
25 Positive expectation
26 Agreement

WHAT'S NEW?

New is **possible**. Just because we did something **yesterday** does not mean we need to do it again today. **Although** it isn't easy, **long-standing** habits can be broken, **alternative** actions taken, and **forgiving** words spoken. We can make **choices** that are unlike those we have made in the past…choices that can turn us in **another direction** and toward the place we want to **find** ourselves in the **future** and the person we **want to become**.

Sometimes **newness** comes in the form of a change in **circumstances**, such as unexpected **opportunity**. But why sit and wait for one? We have the **power** to make things new by **deciding** that we're done with the **old ways** of thinking, **speaking**, acting, and **reacting**. Today we're going to ignore **minor irritations**, let go of **pet peeves**, and say good-bye to sad **memories**. Today we're going to **prove** to ourselves that we are happy, loving, kind, **generous**, and **compassionate**, because we're going to act that way.

Imagine different, **fresh**, **joyful**…and then be it. Let your desire for something **better** express itself. Turn to God, who has said, "I **make all things** new" (Rev. 21:5).

Dear God, help me embrace new, positive, and productive ways of thinking, speaking, and acting.

Discover New

Find the reading's **bolded** words in the word search puzzle.

```
R V T S A L W Y T I N U T R O P P O P B Q U
M R Y W A N T T O B E C O M E C E Z D M Z F
U J E B T C W V V B X H K C Z W S Y I A L D
F S B R E S I D S L H W S U Y B T N K O P C
O P E F U T W R I B X F J Y Z H O R N Z H X
R L Q I H T T O C L W K T Q A R U G J O B P
G X N R R Q U E I U X D W T I W S B I L O G
I L U F Y O J F R J M E M R H T D C N S D N
V V Y S U Z M I D J L S R C A M E L S C H I
I N Y P E C O E H X I I T N B S M I O S H D
N N H E B O A G M J T M D A A X B L X B Z I
G T O I S B V K E A X I A N N L F L H V H C
J S C I A T Z K T N N P E G E C S L G S V E
T G I A T U E I J G E W H E I S E F U X G D
E L P U F C O R U F N R T F G N E S O V W F
Q P S R L N E P D E E A O N R J E X H V D N
H A R E S Z T R S A N V I U W B I K T V D U
Q T D I V M C S I O Y H I C S E V M L K O C
X D D X W E X G I D T S O T E D C C A I M G
E W J P T I E S N L R X J I A R D H B F F N
W S Y N U V S P L I G E K S Y N E V O R P I
M Z D C J A X A T F K E H A D P R W P S Z T
M G B V P I E K Z E S A K T Z D D E O C W C
T S S M I K Q H X J P Y E F O J T N T P X A
N N O R A G F R E S H R C P E N C F I L N E
C C A M H N N H S M A E C G S M A Z F F A R
```

TRADING SHOES

In the Bible, Jesus says, "Do to others as you would have them do to you" (Luke 6:31 niv). The Golden Rule is taught not only in Christianity, but in many other religions, as well. Indeed, it would be difficult to find a person of goodwill who doesn't subscribe to some version of the Golden Rule!

What can be difficult, however, is to practice the Golden Rule in day-to-day life. You can make it easier by imagining yourself in another person's shoes. How would you like to be treated if you were, say, standing behind the counter waiting on customers...driving slowly because you're in an unfamiliar part of town...answering phone calls from a stream of unhappy customers?

The Golden Rule works the other way, too. What if you're the one who's having a bad day and snaps at another person or answers someone sharply? You're grateful when they choose not to take offense...when they're patient with you...when they put themselves in your shoes. It's a golden moment...and maybe that's why it's called the Golden Rule.

*Dear God, help me remember to practice the
Golden Rule whenever I'm among others.*

Matching Pairs

Pick the phrase in the second column that completes the shoe- or feet-related sentence in the first column.

1. In the Upper Room, Jesus washed the feet of...

2. "I'm not worthy to carry His sandals," said...

3. "You're standing on holy ground," said God to...

4. Those who hastily ate the first Passover, with coat and shoes on were the...

5. A man would give his shoe to another to confirm a decision, according to the book of...

6. "Heaven is my throne, Earth my footstool," said...

7. "She washed My feet with her tears and dried them with her hair," said Jesus of...

8. If we walk the path of life with integrity, we will walk securely, according to the book of...

9. It's like a lamp to our feet, says the Psalmist of...

10. The boy who was born grasping the heel of his twin brother was named...

a. Moses

b. Ruth

c. Proverbs

d. a certain woman who led a sinful life

e. His disciples

f. Israelites

g. God's Word

h. John the Baptist

i. Jacob

j. God

Big Puzzler

This puzzle contains many foot- and shoe-related words.

ACROSS

1 Advanced deg.
4 Route
8 Exercise target, maybe
11 __ Grande River
12 Giant
13 Street sign word
14 Frequently, for short
15 Press
16 Scorch
17 Stocking choice, maybe
19 Briny
20 Southwestern Indian
21 Infant
22 Shoe color, perhaps
25 Fizzy drink
26 Dancing shoe
29 Winter shoe
30 Underdone
31 Former Italian currency
32 Note of debt
33 "__ Father"
34 Apes
35 Bone covered by 29 Across
37 "I'll be there in a __" (momentarily)
38 Construction beam material
40 Cobbler's material
44 Descriptor for shoes that fit, e.g.
45 Honey makers
46 To be in debt
47 Spoken
48 Time in office
49 Ocean
50 Dampen
51 __ Major (Big Dipper)
52 Make a mistake

DOWN

1 1 Across, for short
2 Audiophile's choice
3 Speckles
4 Ballet shoes
5 Concur
6 Walk at a fast clip
7 Egg layer
8 Sporting shoe
9 Ferry
10 Active
13 Wound cover
18 Ill-fitting shoes will do this
19 Deplete
21 Curtsy
22 Kimono sash
23 Cry softly
24 Pet
25 Golfer's concern
27 __ of the Covenant

DOWN CON'T

28 Dancer's step
30 Jogger's delight
31 Garret
33 Cooking fat
34 Noxious vapor
36 Shoe part
37 Taunts
38 Skier's delight

39 Car shoe?
40 Smirk
41 Garden need
42 Vessel
43 Back
45 Heat unit

WHERE THE NEEDS ARE

The theologian Martin Luther once noted that "God does not need our good works, but our neighbor does."

God created everything and possesses everything. He certainly has no physical or emotional needs that we can fill for Him. Even more, He loves us completely; there's nothing we can do to earn more love, because we have it all right now. Our "good works"—our service to others, our kindnesses, our compassionate words and helpful actions—are to meet the real, practical, and pressing needs of those around us.

Today, pray. Lift your thoughts to heaven. And then look around you. Go where the needs are.

Dear God, open my eyes to the needs of those around me.

Good Words

Determine the answers to the three clues in each set. If you answered correctly, the forth word will work either before or after each of your answers.

Example:
    Place for canned goods = Pantry
    Fitness, wellbeing = Health
    Heavenly being = Angel
    Answer: Food

1. Exposed = __ __ __

   Beneath = __ __ __ __ __

   Fair, equitable = __ __ __ __

   A: __ __ __ __ __ __

2. Location = __ __ __ __

   Clock's data = __ __ __

   Single = __ __ __

   A: __ __ __

3. Heavily encumbered = __ __ __ __ __ __ __ __

   See to = __ __

   Winter wear = __ __ __ __

   A: __ __ __ __ .

4. Without charge = __ __ __ __

   Fewer = __ __ __ __

   Receiver's opposite = __ __ __ __ __

   A: __ __ __ __

5. Partner = __ __ __ __

   Me = __ __ __ __

   Employed = __ __ __ __ __

   A: __ __ __ __

6. Observing = __ __ __ __ __ __ __

   Resolve = __ __ __ __

   Sense = __ __ __ __

   A: __ __ __ __

7. Adhere to = __ __ __ __ __

   Use the car = __ __ __ __

   Slay = __ __ __ __

   A: __ __ __

8. Abdomen = __ __ __ __

   Cook's broth = __ __ __ __ __

   Car fuel, for short = __ __ __

   A: __ __ __ __ __ __ __

THE DOCTOR IS IN

Those in the medical profession advise us to see our doctor at least once each year. That way, they're able to assess our physical condition and help us remain as healthy as possible. But what we often forget is to regularly check our spiritual health. We do that by comparing our values with our words and actions.

Sometimes the truth isn't pretty. We think we're pretty kind, but then we recall those words we said only yesterday. We believe we help others, but then we remember how often we've been "too busy"...too much in a hurry.

What values do you think you possess...that you want to possess? List them and jot down exactly what you mean. Now take a clear-eyed look at your words and actions over the past six months or so. Do the things you do and say match the things you believe about yourself...about the world...about God?

A physical check-up alerts you to a health problem. Unless you know about it, you can't do something about it! And the same is true with your spiritual well-being.

*Dear God, show me where my words
and actions can more closely match my values.*

Spiritual Check-Up

People in the Bible were real, living people—just like us. They, too, often had difficulty living up to God's expectations; at other times, they were on their best behavior. Match these Bible people with their commendable words or actions.

1. She showed compassion and commitment to her mother-in-law, Naomi, by leaving her own land to follow Naomi to Bethlehem.

2. He readily forgave his brothers for having sold him into slavery when he was a youth.

3. She demonstrated faith by believing the angel Gabriel's message that she would bear the Son of God.

4. Despite a shipwreck, imprisonment, and other hardships, he persevered in spreading the Gospel message.

5. He obeyed God's command to prepare for a great flood, even though there was no rain in sight.

6. She risked her own life to appear before the Persian king unbidden and implement a plan to save her people from Haman's wicked plot.

7. Once his great sin was pointed out to him, he turned to God in heartfelt penitence.

8. She provided generous hospitality to the missionaries who brought her the Gospel message.

9. When God offered him whatever he would want, he asked for wisdom to carry out his duties according to God's will.

10. He made the ultimate sacrifice in atonement for the sins of the world.

a. Joseph
b. David
c. Paul
d. Jesus
e. Esther
f. Lydia
g. Ruth
h. Noah
i. Solomon
j. Mary

SUNNY SIDE UP

Some people seem born with a sunny disposition. They have no trouble seeing the silver lining to any cloud, and looking on the bright side of things comes naturally. For others, however, optimism takes work. Yet it's work well worth doing, because being optimistic enhances life.

Optimism is like a shield that guards you against being disheartened by grumblers and discouraged by naysayers. It's like a ray of light that points the way ahead, even if for only one step at a time. It's like a scale that balances unpleasant realities and present blessings...knotty problems with possible solutions...and finds that the good far outweighs the bad.

Develop the habit of optimism just as you would any other good habit—practice it every day!

Help me, dear God, approach my day with good cheer and an optimistic attitude.

Rhyme Time

Each clue can be answered with two rhyming words.

Example:

Optimist's question to moaner: **W H Y S I G H?**

1. Manager's employees' guffaw:

   _ _ _ _ _ _ _ _ _ _

2. What pessimists do who are afraid of optimism:

   _ _ _ _ _ _ _ _ _ _

3. Lift up joyful worship to God:

   _ _ _ _ _ _ _ _ _ _ _ _

4. Pessimist's no-can-do recitation:

   _ _ _ ' _ _ _ _ _ _ _ _

5. Comedic sweetheart:

   _ _ _ _ _ _ _ _ _ _

6. Enthusiastic high school student:

   _ _ _ _ _ _ _ _ _ _

7. Salve for sorrow:

   _ _ _ _ _ _ _ _ _ _ _

8. Delighted father:

   _ _ _ _ _ _ _ _ _

9. Run away from mirth:

   _ _ _ _ _ _ _ _ _

10. Exam for a jokester:

    _ _ _ _ _ _ _ _ _

11. Very close to optimism:

    _ _ _ _ _ _ _ _ _ _ _

12. The one practicing grins in the mirror is trying to find her personal...:

    _ _ _ _ _ _ _ _ _ _ _ _

13. Thinker of gentle thoughts has one:

    _ _ _ _ _ _ _ _ _ _

14. Sun peeking through dark clouds is one:

    _ _ _ _ _ _ _ _ _ _ _ _

THERE IS MORE

In the quietness of our being, we sense that we are more than the body we live in and the knowledge we possess. We come to realize that material possession cannot adequately fill our most profound longings and that human wisdom cannot fully answer our deepest questions.

Ask God, the one who knows, whether there is more and what it is. Remain open to receiving His gifts of faith and forgiveness, hope and joy, contentment and fulfilment. There is more for you.

Dear God, let me step ahead in faith and trust in You as You fill my deepest yearnings.

The Bible

There are 6 books of the Bible among the answers to this puzzle!

ACROSS

1 Teen condition
5 "To everything there is a season" book (Abbr.)
9 Legion
11 Santa call (2 wds.)
12 Book of the prophet married to Gomer
13 Eastern garment
14 Ephesians (Abbr.)
15 Canadian prov. (Abbr.)
17 Weight unit
18 Small wooden barrel
20 Shout
22 Deface
23 Freemont Street Nevada
24 Jeremiah's book (Abbr.)
27 Black
29 "I am Alpha and __"
31 In addition
32 Exodus mountain
33 KJV "for fear that"
34 Residence hall

DOWN

1. Hurt
2. Harvest
3. Snack
4. Nativity scene critter
5. "Can't hear you!" utterances
6. Raccoon-like animal
7. Book following Kings (Abbr.)
8. Hindquarter
10. Lion's den prophet's book
16. Cheers
18. European country (Abbr.)
19. Distance meas. abroad
20. Type of fur
21. Calvary sight
22. Lunch
24. Comedian Jay
25. Seaweed substance
26. Wound
28. Negative
30. Prefix for city or town

LASTING LUXURIES

When we think of "**luxury** living," we might picture a **palatial** home filled with **expensive** furnishings and **fine** accessories. This is where **someone** lives who takes little notice of the **workaday** world, but glides from **leisurely** mornings and **pleasant** afternoons to **candlelit** evenings and dining **tables** set with **fine china**. No **doubt**, there's luxury living!

Yet more **fulfilling** and more **worthwhile** is another **kind** of luxury living, and it's **available** to **all** of us. By setting **priorities** and **letting go** of the rest, we **provide** ourselves with the luxury of **time** to **pursue** what's most **important**. By focusing on the **present** moment rather than past **regrets** or future **fears**, we give ourselves the luxury of **enjoying** and **delighting** in our daily **blessings**. By offering those around us our full and unhurried attention, we **surround** ourselves with the luxury of meaningful relationships and lasting **friendships**.

While pricey possessions and other **indulgences** might offer the **aura** of luxury living, they **don't deliver**. Hearing the thank-yous... seeing the **smiles** of appreciation...**giving** and **receiving**, serving and **sharing**...having a meaningful **purpose**...knowing you've made a **difference**...those are **lasting** luxuries. At **any time**. In any place.

Dear God, pull my focus away from what I can get
for myself and to what I can give to others.

Living in Luxury

Find the reading's **bolded words** in the word search puzzle.

```
L E T T I N G G O Z J Z P N L A I T A L A P
F Z I T C B N M O E J R N E D R S E L B A T
E L E I S U R E L Y I L D N M U J G A D R P
A A U R K J F C F O N G U S E I Y Y Y P Y E
R D T Y G X Y L R A N O D L I G T D H Q P Z
S A D U M C V I C I R E I O W X N Q W R E U
Z S Q I W W T H Y R L H J I F E N O E M O S
D V P U R I D O U I W S R E S Y M R B B J F
S T Q W E X J S G H F J L S R M Z B K V R C
H E D S C N K H T T J U P R T O Z L T I A P
A F Z X E O T R B H X Z E B E L J N E N R X
R L R T Y I O H U U J V U A O E A N D O B I
I K D C N W K X R A I O R B M S D L V N B M
N B L G L R K Y F L D S L I A S E I S W N P
G P U R S U E J E G E E T E H L D A O A Z O
Q L L A A K P D N C S Y L I I E G R R D H R
E N A U S L T I N S N P P T S N K U S B O T
C E N U N N V E I A Y S Q C I A A E T W E A
N V I A O I G N G X S S O L D W L T E I V N
E C H D E L G O R N G L L A E B S N R Q I T
R C C U S L H T N I I Y S A B M E G D S Q
E A E D A H V Z I M F V O L B K I S E S N G
F R N J R E D T X L O P I L M J L E R Y E Z
F I I E N N S T U N R A B G W J E R Q I P Q
I J F I I A Z F F U V T F J J F S P G H X N
D N F K L G K O P A L X T E S W R T E J E C
```

TREAT YOURSELF

When you give someone a gift, it's a pleasure to see their eyes light up when they open it. That's when you know you've picked just the right thing, and they're delighted not only with the gift, but with the giver. Yet there's someone the happy gift-giver in you might often forget, and that someone is you.

Treat yourself to a little gift every day. Choose to think of something that makes you smile—maybe a happy memory or a much-anticipated occasion. Listen to a song that makes you get up and dance...read a book that takes you to another world...write a poem that expresses your feelings...sketch a scene that brings you joy...call a friend who leaves you encouraged, motivated, inspired. Maybe surprise yourself by walking through your neighborhood as if you've never seen it before. Watch a worthwhile movie quite different than what you would normally choose. Start a conversation with the person next to you in the waiting room...the checkout line... the auditorium before the concert begins.

Little gifts and delightful surprises aren't just for favorite family members, friends, and coworkers. They're for you, too.

Dear God, thank You for the daily gifts
You send to me every day.

Pleasant Surprise

Put the answer to Clue 1 in box 1. Scramble the letters and drop one letter to answer Clue 2. Write the word in box 2 and the dropped letter in the left-hand box. Scramble the letters and drop one letter to answer Clue 3. Write the word in box 3 and the dropped letter in the right-hand box. Complete each row the same way, starting with a new word. When you're finished, you'll discover two new words reading vertically on both sides of the puzzle.

1. Bewail
2. Intended
3. Last word in prayer
4. Hope for
5. Extra, as a tire
6. Church nook
7. Outlines
8. Frighten
9. Too many create a jam
10. Brag
11. Feathery scarves
12. Weep loudly
13. More elevated
14. Not now, but __
15. Genuine
16. Flee from
17. Cloaks
18. Walk back and forth

	1.	2.	3.	
	4.	5.	6.	
	7.	8.	9.	
	10.	11.	12.	
	13.	14.	15.	
	16.	17.	18.	

LASTING GOOD

Perhaps you have heard many stories like these. Tragedy strikes a family, and it is only then that they realize how many caring, compassionate friends and neighbors they have. "Casual acquaintances, even total strangers, stopped to ask how they could help!" a family member exclaims. Or because of a serious illness or serious setback, someone raises public awareness and educates others. Because of that one person's efforts, hundreds if not thousands learn how to cope with their own similar situation.

Loss hurts, and it's a hurt that we will carry in our hearts for as long as we live. Yet from our personal losses often comes boundless good. In our reaching for meaning, for healing, for understanding, we may bless more lives than we could ever know.

There's no quick fix for sorrow, but it's possible that lasting good can come out of it.

Help me, dear God, find ways to turn bad into good.

Comforting Words

Follow the clues by crossing off words in the grid. Some words might be crossed off by more than one clue. When you are finished, you will find words of comfort from Scripture, reading left to right.

1. Cross off all two-letter pronouns.

2. Cross off all words that end with the letter T.

3. Cross off all positive personal qualities.

4. Cross off any books of the Bible.

5. Cross off all words that contain two or more of the same consonants.

6. Cross off all words that start with "com."

7. Cross off all words that mean "three."

8. Cross off all names of musical instruments.

HE	WEST	I	COMFORT
AM	GRATITUDE	JOYFUL	WITH
THRICE	YOU	HORNS	ACTS
ALWAYS	KINDNESS	EVEN	UNTO
TEMPT	THE	US	GOODNESS
REVELATION	HARPS	END	TRINITY
TEST	OF	CONTENTMENT	THE
COMING	WE	CHURCH	TRUMPETS
PATIENCE	MANSION	WORLD	GET

WAYS AND MEANS

We have our own ways of doing things. The way we fix food and stack the plates in the dishwasher...vacuum the floors and fold the laundry...choose what to buy and where to buy it...raise our children and serve our community...we've gone about these common tasks for so long that our way feels like the only way. The right way.

Imagine how many family squabbles and organization arguments could be avoided if we substituted "right" way to "one" way. While what we do might work for us, it might not work as well for others. Plus, watching others perform these tasks differently may let us in on an easier, more efficient, method than the one we've always used. Unless we're participating in a re-enactment of past times, we don't need to hang onto the old ways when something better comes along!

Our "own ways" may serve us well, perhaps even bringing a smile to our lips as we remember watching our parents do the same thing. But their ways, as our ways, are only one of the many ways to raise children...keep a happy home...bring joy and give service to others.

Dear God, thank You for the good and productive ways You have given me to bless those around me.

Way to Go

There are many paths, roads, and highways mentioned in the Bible. Match the road with the people who traveled on it.

1. Road to Emmaus

2. The way from Moab to Judah

3. Road to Damascus

4. Road to Jericho

5. Desert road to the Red Sea

6. An alternate route back to their own country to avoid King Herod in Jerusalem.

7. A narrow path

8. Road from Jerusalem to Gaza.

9. King's Highway

a. Jesus parable of the Good Samaritan took place on it.

b. Ruth accompanied Naomi back to the elder woman's hometown.

c. The Magi chose it after they had visited Jesus, Mary, and Joseph.

d. Jesus said that this way leads to eternal life.

e. The risen Jesus appeared to two of His disciples.

f. Evangelist Philip explained Scriptures to the God-fearing Ethiopian man.

g. Paul was blinded and heard the voice of Jesus speak to him.

h. Route through Edom that the king refused to allow the Israelites to use.

i. It was traveled by the Israelites as they fled Egypt.

Big Puzzler

You may have traveled some of the roads in this puzzle!

ACROSS

3 Pacific __ Highway, California
7 Ad exec's NYC avenue
9 __ Highway, old road from Michigan to Florida
12 Beverly Hills boutique drive
13 Town's thoroughfare
15 Banker's NYC street
17 White House avenue
20 __ Strip, L.A.-area street the locale of former TV series
21 "__ Mile," Chicago's Michigan Avenue

DOWN

1 Houston freeway with 18 lanes of traffic in parts
2 Memphis street of blues singers
4 Appalachian __, stretching from Georgia to Maine
5 Shopper's NYC avenue
6 Starry "Walk of Fame" boulevard
8 Crooked street in San Francisco
10 __ Highway, first road across the U.S.
11 NYC theater thoroughfare
14 __ Street, metaphor for financial well-being
16 New Orleans street that borders historic section
18 __ Trail, pre-railroad way through central North America (2 words)
19 __ 66, storied "Mother Road" from Los Angeles to Chicago

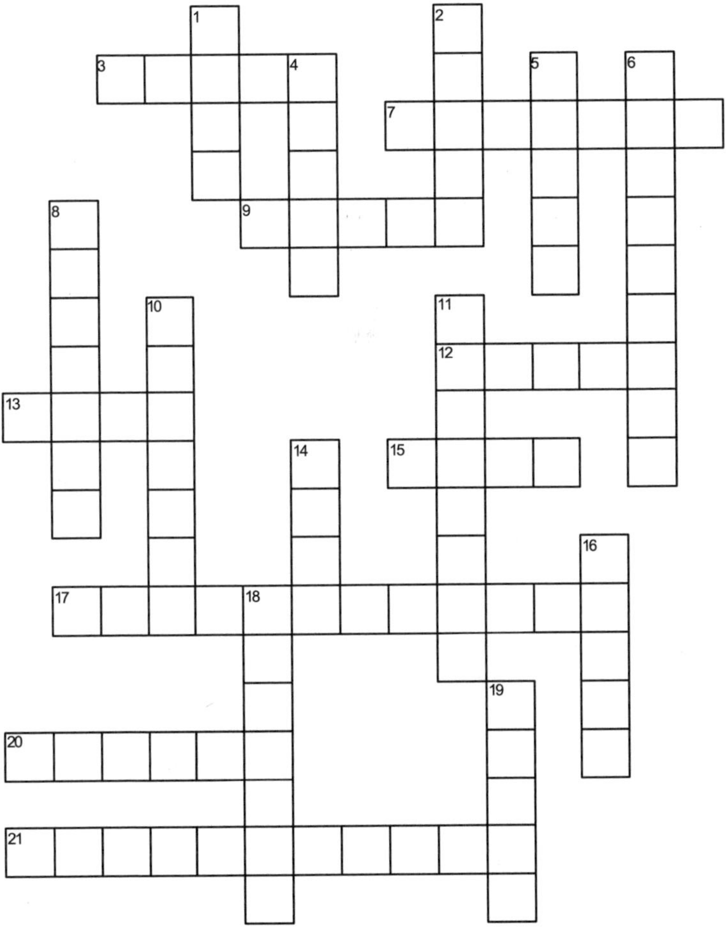
1
2
3
4
5
6
7
8
9
10
11
12
13
14
15
16
17
18
19
20
21

FIRST IMPRESSIONS

We meet some people for the first time and like them immediately. There's something about their appearance, words, or gestures that attracts us, and we look forward to seeing them again and again. At the same time, we meet other people and, right away, decide we don't like them at all. Perhaps they've said nothing more to us than "hello," yet we have no desire to get to know them better.

First impressions are real, and we can't avoid them; but we need not make them permanent. Perhaps the person who comes across as friendly, outgoing, and sociable finds it difficult to maintain deep, long-term relationships. A fast-friendship may result in disappointment. Maybe the one who, upon first meeting, seems nervous and withdrawn is simply shy and needs someone to express interest by extending a warm welcome and friendly smile. A quick dismissal of this person based on our first impression could find us walking away from a fascinating individual.

There's so much more to each of us than any first impression—positive or negative—can possibly convey. We all deserve another look, don't we?

Dear God, I want to be fair to everyone I meet by getting beyond my first impression.

Hidden Words

Give another look, and within each sentence, you'll find the hidden words listed below.

Example: TAP   EARS   RAN   TOME

It appears st**ran**ge **to me**.

MINE	DAD	LOVE	CENT	TIRE
PEND	LIED	FEST	BULL	DIN
TOUR	CORD	SCRIPT	CARE	LAY
DOUR	RED	SCAN	EAR	THE
RIFT	PORT	SLAY	AIRY	NEAR
SOY	STOVE	GAIN	DIFFER	FUSE
REF	ATE	RAT	REST	KIN
TEND	TONE	NEIGH	OUT	RACE

1. "Roll over, Fido!" urged my neighbor as the ebullient puppy complied.

2. He played the accordion at our fall festival this year.

3. The luminescent portrait arrested our attention.

4. If useful, expenditures can extend into next week.

5. Take a different route so you get back in time.

6. Is the test over yet, and did Peter ace it again?

7. He drifted from one area to another before finding his place.

8. Was layered cake entirely eaten?

9. The dairy included a description of her career.

YES

Have you ever been hesitant to, say, ask a friend for a favor? Apply for a job? Try out for a team? Wonder if you can dance, sing, be happier?

If you never attempt it, the answer is "No." Give yourself a chance to explore something new. Sure, the answer might be "No," but in all probability, it will be "Yes, of course you can."

Go ahead and give it a try.

Help me, dear God, overcome my fear of trying something I would like to do.

Things to Try

You may discover many things you'd like to try in this puzzle!

ACROSS

1 Swift animals
5 Scott Joplin compositions
9 Visual
11 Zion National Park state
12 Singer's voice, maybe
13 Call
14 You might want to sail it
15 M.S. evaluator
17 Commanded
18 Lifts
20 You can strum one
22 Friend
23 Chicago's transport, for short
24 Beret
27 Exits
29 Comment on
31 Old Testament book
32 Accra's locale
33 Make reference to
34 Female 1 Across

DOWN

1. You can connect them
2. Fencer's sword
3. Gas burner
4. ___ Grande
5. Join a marathon, e.g.
6. Dickens' "___ of Two Cities" (2 wds.)
7. Sports
8. Outbuilding, maybe
10. Invent
16. Conversation
18. East Coast state (Abbr.)
19. Jr.'s dad
20. Netting
21. Supreme (Prefix)
22. Verse
24. "Bye-bye"
25. Jesus' grandmother, by tradition
26. Legumes
28. ___ Francisco
30. Advanced degree

A WORD TO THE WOUNDED

Sometimes we just don't know what to say. Work-worn phrases of caring and sympathy can't express the depth of our feelings when someone hurts, and only sound weak and ineffectual when they cross our lips. But we utter them anyway, hoping that our grieving loved one, our heartbroken friend, will know what we mean.

And, yes, they know. While they might not be able to recall exactly the words you used, they'll remember the soothing, reassuring sound of your voice. Later, they'll think back to the comfort of your presence and whisper a heartfelt thank you for what you did... how you took time out of your busy afternoon to visit with them... how you didn't try to push away their sorrow, but listened as they told you, perhaps for the umpteenth time, how much they hurt... how you were there for them when they needed someone to care.

Your words matter, of course. But there's no need to fish for unique or original phrases when what matters most of all is that you are there.

Dear God, let me be the one who is fully present when my friends and loved ones need me.

Words of Prayer

God invites us to pray for those who are grieving or struggling, and there are many examples throughout the Bible. Match those who prayed with their petition.

1. Hannah

    a. This missionary prayed that God would remove an ailment he called a "thorn in the flesh."

2. Abraham

    b. He prayed to Jesus that He would restore his little daughter who had died.

3. Stephen

    c. In the temple, this distraught woman prayed for a baby, and God blessed her with a son, Samuel.

4. Paul

    d. He prayed that God would provide a way across the Red Sea and away from pursuing Egyptians.

5. Moses

    e. This king prayed for wisdom rather than ask for wealth and glory.

6. David

    f. He prayed for forgiveness for leaving his father's house and wasting his inheritance.

7. Jesus' disciples

    g. He bargained with God in hopes that enough God-fearing people lived in Sodom to save it.

8. Solomon

    h. Fearful for their lives, they prayed during a storm on the Sea of Galilee.

9. Jairus

    i. This evangelist prayed that God would forgive those who were stoning him.

10. Prodigal son

    j. He prayed for forgiveness for an adulterous relationship and for bringing about a murder.

WHAT ARE YOU THINKING?

If you want to reduce clutter in your home, you know what to do—sell, recycle, or toss those things that no longer serve their purpose. They once were useful, fun, functional, or life-enriching, but they don't meet your present needs or interests. Maybe some possessions were poor choices from the beginning; time isn't going to change their value to you. All this is clutter you can get rid of.

The mind, too, collects clutter. Patterns of thinking that repeatedly have led to failure...visions of the future based on exaggerated fears or unrealistic hopes...hurts, regrets, and mistakes of the past that weigh down the heart and darken today. Just as with unneeded things around your home, all this is clutter you can get rid of!

*Help me get rid of those thoughts, dear God,
that keep me from living fully and joyfully.*

It's the Thought That Counts

The Bible contains many thoughts about thoughts! Each verse below, however, has a missing "thought" or two. Complete the sentences with words from the box below (all words will be used once).

HONEST	NIGHT	THINKING	HEARTS
GIVE	MY	VIRTUE	WORKS
ESTABLISHED	WEIGHS	WAYS	WHICH
FALL	THOUGHT	DISCERNER	HEART
NOT	THINGS	FIRM	KNEW
GENERATIONS	MEDITATE	COUNSEL	REPORT

SEARCH	COMMIT	DELIGHT	TOWARD
RIGHT	ONE	WAYS	ANY
CAREFUL	EVIL	INTENTS	

1. My thoughts are _____ your thoughts, neither are your _____ my _____ , saith the Lord. (Isaiah 55:8)

2. Whatsoever things are true, whatsoever things are _____, whatsoever things are just, whatsoever things are pure, whatsoever things are lovely, whatsoever things are of good _____ ; if there be any _____, and if there be _____ praise, think on these things. (Philippians 4:8)

3. I know the thoughts that I think _____ you, saith the Lord, thoughts of peace, and not of _____, to _____ you an expected end. (Jeremiah 29:11)

4. The _____ of the Lord standeth forever, the thoughts of his heart to all _____ . (Psalm 33:11)

5. _____ of you with taking _____ can add to his stature _____ cubit? (Luke 12:25)

6. A person may think their own ways are _____ , but the Lord _____ the heart. (Proverbs 21:2 niv)

7. His _____ is in the law of the Lord; and in his law doth he _____ day and _____ . (Psalm 1:2)

8. If you think you are standing _____ , be _____ that you don't _____ ! (1 Corinthians 10:12 niv)

9. _____ me, O God, and know my _____ : try me, and know _____ thoughts. (Psalm 139:23)

10. _____ thy _____ unto the Lord, and thy thoughts shall be _____ . (Proverbs 16:3)

11. The word of God...is a _____ of the thoughts and _____ of the heart. (Hebrews 4:12)

12. Jesus _____ what they were _____ and asked, "Why are you thinking these _____ in your _____?" (Luke 5:22 niv)

KEEPERS

Decluttering by itself is only half the story. The other half is about keeping.

Some possessions are functional and make your daily life more comfortable. Others you keep because of the beauty, pleasure, or memories they bring. Perhaps you have additional reasons for keeping the things you do.

The same holds true for the possessions of your mind and heart. Do your "keepers" bless your life? If so, they are well worth keeping!

Thank You, dear God, for blessing my life with so many treasures, in my home and in my heart.

Keep What You Love

This puzzle is full of keepers of all kinds!

ACROSS

- 5 You have it when you play
- 6 Allegiance
- 8 Recollections
- 10 Heart's emotion
- 11 They might be right there or online
- 15 Conversation with God
- 16 Belief in God
- 18 Positive outlook
- 21 You're wished sweet ones at night
- 22 It puts a bounce in your step
- 23 Amazement
- 24 They're great to recall (2 words)
- 25 Loveliness

DOWN

1. Worth
2. Exaltation
3. Marvel
4. Rely on
5. Household members, most often
7. Ecstasy
9. "Tickled pink" feeling
12. Grin
13. Reason, as to do something
14. Ingenuity
17. Delectation
19. Inner contentment
20. Expectation

🍀 LIFE-CHANGER

Faith in God is life-changing, and here's why. When you believe in His presence, you are shielded from the feeling that you're all alone in the world; you're not. He is always with you. When you rely on His power, you're free from the burden of thinking everything depends on you. It doesn't; you have His strength and His power to lean on.

When you accept His wisdom as knowledge far above yours, you're able to entrust your burdens to His will. This opens your heart and mind to discover deeper truths and positive solutions. When you humbly consent to His timing, you grow in patience, knowing that He will make all things work out for you. When you converse with Him in prayer, you are recognizing that He is real... that He hears...that He cares.

As someone who believes in God, you naturally want to meet other people of faith. This puts you among people who can encourage you, and you get to do the same for them. Now you have a support group!

Faith is life-changing because God has the desire and the power to change lives. How has He changed yours?

Transformations

Change the first word into the second word of each pair by replacing only one letter at a time. Do not scramble letter order; use only common English words, and no capitalized words.

Example:

> LOSE
> lone
> line
> fine
> FIND

1. HURT

   _____
   _____
   _____
   _____

   CALM

2. FEAR

   _____
   _____
   _____
   _____

   PRAYER

3. STAY

   _____
   _____
   _____
   _____

   FREE

4. REAL

   _____
   _____
   _____
   _____

   LIFE

5. TRUE

   _____
   _____
   _____
   _____

   LOVE

GOOD RELATIONS

Our **relationships** are like gardens—they **flourish** only when we **nurture** them. It doesn't matter what kind of relationship we're **talking about**. Family, **friend**, church, **workplace**, and community connections become **significant**, grow **strong**, and remain **vital** only with constant **care**.

"**Weeds**" take over when we take our relationships for **granted**... get so **involved** in our own **goals** and **interests** that we **neglect** the **presence** of others...focus so much on **entertainment** and **social** media that we have **little time** for the **loved one** sitting right in front of us.

Fortunately, keeping the "weeds" **away** from our "gardens" is a **pleasant** and **joyful** experience. Giving in-the-moment **attention** to those around us **keeps** us **aware** of others' needs and **feelings**, and then we can provide practical **help** and **encouragement**. That's how our own lives **blossom** with **purpose** and **meaning**! Participating with others in **positive** activities creates the **kind** of relationships that, like well-tended gardens, add **beauty** to the day and **sunshine** to the **heart**.

Dear God, let me always be thankful for my relationships, and take time to nuture them.

Vital Connections

Find the reading's **bolded** words in the word search puzzle.

```
U N D N E I R F G W E E D S O I V U A F T G
H V M Z G K E E P S R H L P N J J Q O S R S
U A E K J L U F Y O J G N O R T S R P A I M
V D M K P B E A U T Y S G E M M T D N G B S
N W I U Z D E V A Z Z V C O D U Z T N T O H
F O T E E P H B Q I E V S H N T E I R C K S
B R E E C N E S E R P S E A V D F A I G U K
O K L S L P D K Z U O L T X E I E A G N S C
D P T B O G T S J L P E Q N C H L Y S L A Z
R L T N L G H M B G L Y O A H T M H X R J A
K A I E G K Z W N Y D D N T C S I Z E Y W O
Z C L G N U R T U R E T G U M N I O G A O P
T E N L B Z W J C V Y P G O E E H R R W B R
X T T E G B D C O D M S S B E N A E U A U F
P N P C Z O G L E R P P L A F V Y N Z O E T
W E E T Z Q A V I S U I E G O P I H I E L H
B M X C O R L L H Y R H D N A W I T L N N F
O E F P Z O B C S G P S Q I P M W I I I G E
T G W T V X V X K S O N M K I W N K P S P O
B A P N J N A C V Y S O J L U G P X W G O L
X R I A O D Z M V L E I O A S D R H X S U P
T U P S H D L L A G L T K T O I E V C P Z Z
X O S A I T X B A A M A B N O I T N E T T A
N C G E D N I K T S T L G A B X V J E L K X
E N Q L Z M B I E N T E R T A I N M E N T I
Y E F P K T V I N T E R E S T S M M S G U P
```

TRUE TO YOU

When we hear the world "loyalty," it's usually in connection with loyalty to a country, or to a cause, or to his family, or to the people in her workplace. Loyal people lend the best of their time and talents to the object of their loyalty, and they do everything they can to support and defend it. How often, however, do we hear about loyalty to ourselves?

We're loyal to ourselves when we remain true to ourselves by saying, in the kindest and most appropriate way, what we really think rather than echoing someone else's words...choosing, whenever possible, what brings joy to our heart, even if it is not the choice of those around us...doing what reflects our best selves instead of taking the path of least resistance.

Self-loyalty takes introspection—you have to know yourself!—yet it's essential for anyone who wants to live as an authentic person. For all who are brave enough to stand for something worthwhile, and courageous enough to defend it in the face of opposition. It's essential for you.

Dear God, help me discover where my true loyalties lie.

Loyal, Disloyal

Loyalty is a choice. Choose the correct answer to these Bible questions about loyalty—and its opposite!

1. This prince's loyalty to his friend, David, compelled him to tell David of his father's murderous intentions and make possible David's escape.
   a. Samuel
   b. Jonathan
   c. Absalom

2. This woman's disloyalty to her husband caused the downfall of one of Israel's warriors.
   a. Delilah
   b. Jezebel
   c. Gomer

3. When this young man abandoned a mission trip, he caused a rift between Paul and Barnabas:
   a. Timothy
   b. Titus
   c. John Mark

4. Her loyalty to the Israelites was affirmed when she deceived and then killed an enemy commander, Sisera:
   a. Hannah
   b. Delilah
   c. Jael

5. This mother's loyalty to God and her promise to Him was confirmed when she presented her son to Eli the priest:
   a. Sarah
   b. Hannah
   c. Mary

6. This disciple's loyalty to Jesus was severely tested, and failed, when a servant-girl asked him if he was a disciple of Jesus:
   a. Thomas
   b. John
   c. Peter

7. This disciple's loyalty to Jesus compelled him to stand at the foot of Jesus' cross:
   a. John
   b. James
   c. Matthew

8. This uncle of Esther encouraged her to remain loyal to her own people, even though it could mean death for her:
   a. Haman
   b. Ahasuerus
   c. Mordecai

9. This Levite led an unsuccessful rebellion against the leadership of Moses and Aaron:
   a. Korah
   b. Joshua
   c. Achan

10. This man's loyalty to his family compelled him to forgive his brothers' past treachery:
    a. Moses
    b. Joseph
    c. Cain

WHAT IF?

How long has it been since you've asked yourself, "What if?" When you were growing up, you might have spent many lazy summer afternoons lying on the grass, looking up at the clouds, and wondering, "What if I could sail away on a cloud?"... "What if I could swing on a star?"

Certainly many "what ifs" are merely whimsical daydreams and imaginative fancies. They make you smile, and that's not such a bad thing, is it? But then again, you'll never know what's possible... what you'd really like to do...what amazing, delightful, and wonderful thing can happen if you never stop to ask, "What if?"

Dear God, grant me the gift of being able to ask, "What if?"

Good Questions

Many men and women in the Bible were not afraid to ask for what they wanted, even when their request might have seemed impossible. Match the name in the list with the question the person asked; each name will be used only once.

GIDEON	BARTIMAEUS	THIEF ON THE CROSS	ELIJAH
PAUL	MARTHA	REBEKAH	SARAH
MOSES	HEZEKIAH	JABEZ	JAIRUS

1. He asked for someone to speak for him in front of Pharaoh, claiming a speech impediment.

2. He prayed for more time on Earth, and God added 15 years to his life.

3. He placed a wool fleece on the threshing floor and asked God for a sign that he could lead Israel to a victory; God answered his request.

4. Abraham's servant prayed that the young woman who extended hospitality to him would be the one God intended for Isaac's bride, and God caused this woman to welcome him.

5. He prayed for the removal of a disability, but God replied that His grace was sufficient for him.

6. She had given up hope of ever conceiving, and when the Lord announced that she would bare a son, she laughed.

7. She begged Jesus to come to her home quickly so He could heal her ailing brother. Jesus allowed Lazarus to die, but then increased her faith by raising him from the grave.

8. He begged Jesus to come to his home and heal his daughter, who had died; and He returned life to her.

9. This blind beggar pleaded with Jesus to restore his sight, and Jesus granted his request on account of his faith.

10. This man prayed that God would bless his work and enlarge his territory, and God did exactly that.

11. This man asked Jesus for forgiveness, and Jesus assured him that he would be with Him in paradise.

12. He prayed that God would show His sovereign power by producing flames on an altar he had built, alongside an altar the worshipers of Baal had built. God sent a consuming fire.

Big Puzzler

Relax and enjoy solving this crossword puzzle!

ACROSS

1 Affirms
6 South American nation
10 Big __, London landmark
13 Limited
15 Cry of dismay
16 Paris street
17 New Testament Roman ruler
18 Ride the waves
19 Fall mo.
20 Gardener's medium
22 Fill with joy
24 Jesus, the __ Shepherd
26 Operator
28 Challenge
29 Damage
30 Happy
31 Filleted
32 Pie __ mode (2 words)
33 Swift
34 Computer Keyboard key
35 Tropical malady
37 Have
41 Movie scene
42 Canter
43 Deer cousin
44 Tent fastener
47 Winged
48 Work's opposite
49 Domicile
50 Word book (Abbr.)
51 Fastener
52 Creative products
54 Seers
56 English Title
57 River dam
59 Resurrection Day
63 Beverage
64 Zilch
65 Formal agreement
66 Query
67 Air pollution
68 Ceasefire

DOWN

1 Athletic org.
2 By way of
3 Solo
4 What Solomon had
5 Sedate
6 Dads
7 Got away from
8 Less common
9 '80s athletic org.
10 Coarse ankle high - work shoe

DOWN CON'T
11 Card game
12 Got as profit
14 Sin
21 City in Oklahoma
23 Baals
24 Big celebration
25 Spoken
27 Rested
29 Noah's son
30 Stride
31 Top-notch
33 Without cost
34 Portal
36 Crooked
37 Chatter
38 Snaky fish
39 Strike
40 Heavens
42 Nurse's trait, for short
44 Cascade mountain
45 Early American British supporters
46 Commuter train company
47 Japanese martial art
48 Quarterback
50 Imagine
51 Chest thumper
53 Has
55 Still
58 Cleaning cloth
60 Greek letter
61 List ender
62 Bread choice

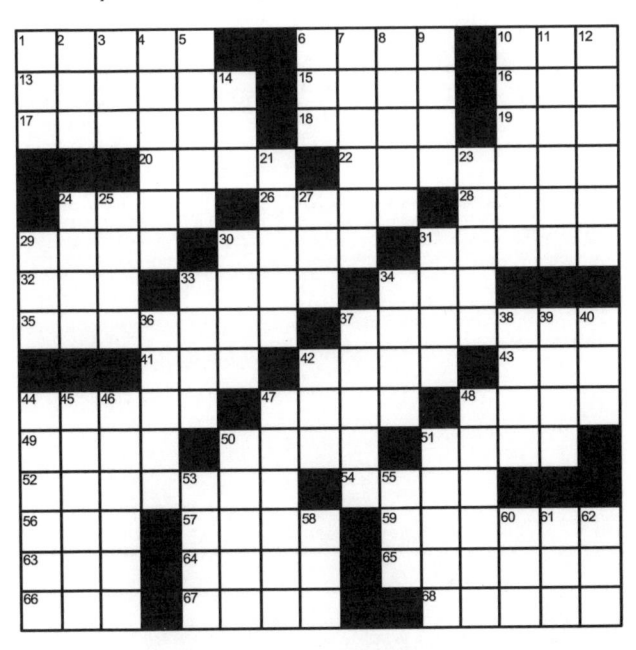

SOMETHING NEW

When you go on vacation to a place you've never been, you notice things. In a big city, you might tip your head back to glimpse the tops of skyscrapers, or stand gazing at the decorative facades of churches and government buildings. In rural areas, perhaps your eyes would sweep wide-open fields from horizon to horizon. At the beach, who hasn't felt the majesty of crashing waves, or delighted in the way the sun's rays skitter across the water? These are just a few of the things you might talk about when you get back home!

But you don't need to pack your bags and head to an exotic destination to savor interesting sights and amazing scenery. You can do the same thing right, as they say, in your own backyard. Simply look around you as if you're seeing things for the very first time. Notice the architecture, the landscape, and the sky. Describe your location to yourself as if you're telling someone who has never been there.

You're sure to discover something new, minus the cost of a plane ticket!

Dear God, grant me eyes to see all the beauty around me.

Happy Discoveries

Put the answer to Clue 1 in box 1. Scramble the letters and drop one letter to answer Clue 2. Write the word in box 2 and the dropped letter in the left-hand box. Scramble the letters and drop one letter to answer Clue 3. Write the word in box 3 and the dropped letter in the right-hand box. Complete each row the same way, starting with a new word. When you're finished, you'll discover two new words reading vertically on both sides of the puzzle.

1. Clutch
2. Exchange blows
3. Knock
4. Extols
5. Church peaks
6. Iron
7. Browsed, as sheep
8. School level
9. Challenge
10. KJV "yours"
11. Slim
12. Louse
13. Ogle
14. Fee per hour
15. Time period

	1.	2.	3.	
	4.	5.	6.	
	7.	8.	9.	
	10.	11.	12.	
	13.	14.	15.	

FEELING FINE

On days when our responsibilities seem heavy and burdensome, we often wish we could simply please ourselves and do only what we feel like doing. That's instead of jumping out of bed as soon as the alarm clock sounds...putting in a full day at work...looking after kids or meeting the needs of others. Yet if we were free to follow our feelings day after day, our lives would quickly lose meaning and purpose. The more we'd try to grasp happiness and fulfillment, it would elude us. Why? Because feelings are fleeting.

Feelings change at will, leading us one day in one direction, the next day in another. For instance, feelings of love, without commitment as a foundation, dissipate with time....enthusiasm, minus perseverance, wanes as the thrill of newness wears off...happiness, unless it resides in the heart, depends solely on whatever is going on around us.

Let your feelings enhance your life...but not plot its course. Let them open you to the depth and breadth of human experience...but not displace enduring values. Let positive, uplifting feelings bless your day...just as God intended.

*Dear God, teach me how my feelings can bless
my life with true and lasting joy.*

An Emotional Response

Match the Bible name in the first column with his or her feelings and response in the second column.

1. Joseph

2. Ruth

3. Rueben

4. Paul

5. Abraham

6. Stephen

7. Felix

8. Elijah

9. Lydia

10. Jonah

a. This Old Testament prophet was depressed because he felt that he was the only one left who believed in the true God.

b. Fear for his safety led this patriarch to present Sarah as his sister instead of his wife.

c. This Old Testament prophet became angry when God forgave the people of a wicked city rather than destroy the city.

d. His devotion to his fiancée caused him to consider quietly breaking their engagement rather than publicly shame her because of her pregnancy.

e. This governor's feeling that he could listen to the Gospel message at a later, more convenient time led him to dismiss Paul.

f. This apostle's reliance on God gave him contentment, regardless of his particular circumstances.

g. Her compassion compelled her to accompany her mother-in-law into a foreign land and see to her survival.

h. This woman from Thyatira was so happy to hear the Gospel message that she opened her home to Paul and his companions.

i. His commitment to the Gospel allowed him to see heaven opened while he was being stoned to death.

j. His guilty feelings prompted him to rescue his younger brother, but before he could, his other brothers sold the young man into slavery.

IT'S ONLY A NUMBER

Maybe it is the first sign of gray hair, or the birth of a grandchild, or a "milestone" birthday that stops us short. Are we really that old? Yet we don't feel old inside. In fact, we feel little different than we did, say, ten, twenty, or even thirty years ago. Oh, perhaps a few aches and pains we've never had before, but we're still "us." Now we understand what the eighty-year-olds, ninety-year-olds, one-hundred-year-olds, mean when they say, "It's only a number."

The passing years invite us to grow deeper in understanding, wisdom, and spirituality. Our changing lives bring us to realize what's really important—and it's not the smoothness of our skin, the swiftness of our gait, or even our past or present personal power or social status. What's important are those things that increase with time, such as our ability to experience joy...our willingness to give thanks...our sense of peace and contentment...our readiness to laugh and smile and play.

What's most important is inside you, and ready to be nourished, cultivated, and lived to the fullest. Everything else is only a number.

Dear God, thank You for the gift of years.

Count 'Em!

Choose the right answer for each question about numbers in the Bible.

1. How many books are in the King James Version of the Bible?
   a. 36
   b. 66
   c. 86

2. How many days did water remain on Earth including the 40 days and 40 nights of rain?
   a. 90
   b. 150
   c. 365

3. How many days did Jonah remain in the body of the great fish God had sent to him?
   a. 3
   b. 7
   c. 12

4. How many original tribes of Israel were there in the Old Testament?
   a. 10
   b. 12
   c. 33

5. When Jesus rose from the tomb on Easter morning, how many days did He remain on Earth?
   a. 3
   b. 12
   c. 40

6. How many times were the disciples to forgive others, according to Jesus?
   a. 70 x 7
   b. 12 x 12
   c. 144

7. How many men did Moses send to spy on the land of Canaan?
   a. 2
   b. 12
   c. 40

8. How many people were in the ark during the Great Flood?
   a. 8
   b. 12
   c. 33

9. How many years did Israel spend in exile in Babylon?
   a. 70
   b. 700
   c. 1,000

10. After Jesus' resurrection, how many days was it until Pentecost?
    a. 30
    b. 40
    c. 50

A BEAUTIFUL YOU

What would it take to add something beautiful to your day? You might think of buying a bouquet of flowers, but it's true that flowers can cost a pretty penny...or painting a lovely picture, but you might never have picked up an artist's brush in your life...or savoring music that enchants you, but with all you have to do, there might not be time to sit down and listen to it.

Fortunately, it takes neither money nor special talent nor leisure time to add beauty to any day. It's all free, and you can do it wherever you are. All you need is a beautiful attitude, and it will blossom naturally into a warm smile for the people around you...a friendly greeting for the cashier at the checkout counter...a thoughtful gesture for a friend...kind and gentle words for your loved ones.

These things, though they take only a moment of your time, have the power to brighten someone's perspective...build a sense of trust and self-worth...strengthen the ties of friendship...create peace in the home...and make the world more beautiful. Like the way you'll feel all day long.

Help me, dear God, choose a beautiful attitude today and every day.

Echoes

Each clue can be answered with two rhyming words. All refer to a something of beauty, and the spaces show how many letters are in the answer.

Example: Compassionate mentality   K I N D   M I N D

1. Squad's ray of sunshine

___ ___

2. Refined, beautiful area

____ ____

3. Heavenly smooch

____ ___

4. Grin trend

____ ____

5. Fresh outlook

___ ____

6. Pleasant getaway spot

____ _____

7. Intelligent chest-thumper

____ ____

8. Pious yell

_____ ____

9. Pleasant glow

___ ____

10. Eye-twinkle connection

___ ___

111

🌿 LIGHT AND DARK

The skillful use of light and dark makes the difference between a simple picture and a captivating work of art. One without the other—dark without light, or light without dark—may make a statement, but doesn't tell a complete story.

Life is a mix of light and dark. How could you truly experience one without the other? God, the consummate artist, has designed a meaningful story for you. Never fear the dark, because He is there. Bask in the light for the same reason—He is there.

Dear God, let the reality of Your presence give me joy.

Color Your World

You'll find many "colorful" clues in this crossword puzzle!

ACROSS

1 Chew
5 Centers
9 Extremely wealthy person
11 On a cruise
12 Orange
13 Business wear
14 Oolong
15 Ouch!
17 Era
18 Breathe in
20 Unleavened breads
22 Chemist's meas.
23 Chicago transport, for short
24 Tint
27 Light brown
29 Black
31 Negatives
32 Dark gray
33 Colors
34 Walked

DOWN

1 Annoying insect
2 Label
3 "Whereby we cry, __, Father" (Rom. 8:15)
4 Trouble
5 Owns
6 Customary
7 Off-white
8 Fill
10 Yellow-brown
16 Complete items
18 Programmer's dept.
19 Like
20 "The Real __"
21 Jibe
22 Patch
24 Gray-white
25 "Come __ me, all ye that labour" (Matt. 11:28)
26 Leered
28 Ship initials
30 Deli order, for short

IT'S OBVIOUS

Some things are obvious, like the beauty of a fragrant garden... the tranquility of a sheltered pond...the contentment of a loving couple. And then other things are not obvious at all, like the whys and wherefores of what often takes place in the world...or even what makes a cell phone work!

There are some verses and events in the Bible whose meaning is not obvious at all. Across millennia, theologians have delved deeply into Scripture, yet some passages still defy human understanding. Perhaps God, through the mysteries of Scripture, invites us to keep searching, keep exploring, keep coming to Him, keep asking questions and looking for answers.

The Bible's most important message, however, is crystal clear. God makes His continuing and unchangeable love for us obvious. He doesn't hide His compassion, His mercy, and His readiness to forgive. He plainly points us to Jesus, our Savior, guiding us to faith in Him.

When you open the Bible, let God make His love for you obvious. Let His love become part of your life.

Open my eyes, dear God, to the love You have for me.

Hidden Words

Give another look, and within each sentence, you'll find the hidden words listed below.

Example: TAP   EARS   RAN   TOME

It **ap**pears st**ra**nge **to me**.

DINT	SHIMMY	TALENT	LED	SEA
WEST	TRIES	OWNER	CHASE	MESH
HAM	NORM	PIN	RING	USE
LIVE	GONE	NINTH	DAB	ASH
SIT	HERMIT	WET	SISAL	WHERE
RED	ONLY	PART	VERY	THERE
SALSA	TORE	EDITOR	RAGE	FIT

1. Her mittens were daringly worn in the house.

2. When we stay in town, Erda asks to review her entries.

3. If it pleases him, my happiness is always enormous.

4. "Deliver me!" she yelled as I dashed into her apartment.

5. Has Al Sanders rented it, or is it purchased from the repo garage?

6. What a Lenten season! Lying on Earl's hammock, we talked about everything.

IN THE KNOW

Experts are people who know their subject backward and forward. Perhaps they have put in many years of study, or they've been practicing for decades, or they've spent countless hours analyzing data, pouring over information, and comparing notes with others. When you have a question or need information, an expert on the topic is the one you want to ask!

Many of us, however, don't regard ourselves as experts, even though we might be managing a household...raising children...enjoying a career...tracking an athletic team...perfecting a specific skill...reading books...following a TV series...keeping up with musical trends...traveling...pursuing lifelong education. OK, so maybe we're not the kind of experts invited to speak in front of vast audiences, but we sure know a lot about our subject!

Let others in on what you do and what you're good at. It makes for engaging conversation. And you might be surprised at the number of times someone says, "Wow! That's so interesting, because I've always wanted to ask..." And you might astonish yourself to realize that you know the answer backward and forward—because you're the expert.

Dear God, let me be generous in sharing my knowledge and experience with others.

Backward and Forward

Palindromes are words that can be read forward or backward—words like "bib" or "stats." The answer to each clue in this puzzle is a palindrome. The number of spaces corresponds to the number of letters in the word.

1. Pasture grazer

___ ___ ___

2. Slender paddle boat

___ ___ ___ ___ ___

3. Opera arias

___ ___ ___ ___ ___

4. Fast automobile

___ ___ ___ ___ ___   ___ ___ ___ ___

5. Principle or precept

___ ___ ___ ___ ___

6. Equal

___ ___ ___ ___ ___

7. Mention, with "to"

___ ___ ___ ___ ___

8. Admonition not to move the head up and down

___ ___ ___ ___,' ___ ___   ___ ___ ___ ___

9. Public, often with "duty"

___ ___ ___ ___ ___

10. More crimson

___ ___ ___ ___ ___ ___

11. Shoulder part, with "cuff"

___ ___ ___ ___ ___ ___ ___

12. Order to throw out wet soil

___ ___ ___ ___   ___ ___ ___

117

THREE LITTLE WORDS

Three words, sincerely spoken, can pack a lot of meaning. "I love you" encapsulates a wide range of deeply held feelings and the promise of long-lasting devotion and loyalty. "I am sorry" renews friendships and restores ties between people. "Thank You, God" gives credit to the giver of all good gifts, reminding us not only from whom our blessings come, but the source of our very life and breath.

"You were great" and "You did well" are three words that recognize achievements, however small, and encourage effort and excellence. An honest "I don't know" far surpasses a torrent of words to cover up a lack of knowledge. A simple "Let me help" lifts more hearts than a long list of excuses...or a neglectful, louder-than-words silence.

Say "Let me try," and then put your heart and mind to the task without telling others not to expect much. Think "I am worthy," because no one's life is without God-given value and purpose. Remember "God is love," because those three words will strengthen you in difficulties, comfort you in sorrow, and support you always.

What more is there to say?

> *Dear God, let the words I speak reflect kindness, meaning, and truth.*

Three-Letter Words

Each answer in this puzzle is short and sweet—only three letters long!

ACROSS

1. Everyone
4. The Caribbean is one
7. Luau dish
8. Wise bird
9. Tide movement
10. One introduced to society, for short
11. Duet
14. Epoch
17. Pasture sound
18. Cavity
19. Query
20. Cheat

DOWN

1. Jungle critter
2. Toss
3. Ad __
4. Ground
5. Ram's mate
6. Priestly vestment
11. Information to come, for short
12. Used to be
13. Mighty tree
14. Chick holder
15. Sunbeam
16. Tablet download

CAN'T BE HELPED

When you meet certain people, you just have to smile. The bounce to their step...the twinkle in their eyes...the easy, lighthearted lilt in their voice. Right away, you know they have a friendly, feel-good sense of humor.

It doesn't take the ability to tell jokes at the spur of the moment, have a snappy comeback always at the ready, or add a witty observation to every topic. In fact, verbal pranks can intimidate, even offend, others when they're delivered without regard to time or place. This humor often repels, rather than attracts, people.

A sense of humor that uplifts others is, first of all, kind. It takes no victims and inflicts no harm. Second, it considers the feelings of others. Rather than trying to jolly-up a heavy heart, it simply offers the hope and comfort that a positive perspective brings. Third, a genuine sense of humor comes from the heart. When you feel good about yourself, you feel good about others; and when you feel good about others, you feel good about the world. And when you feel good about the world, there's a bounce to your step...a twinkle in your eyes...and an easy, lighthearted lilt to your voice. You just can't help it!

Grant me, dear God, a sense of humor that invites, uplifts, and encourages others.

How Funny!

Though we don't think of the Bible as a funny book, there's humor scattered throughout its pages. Match the incident in the first column with the person in the second column.

1. To illustrate how each person possesses unique gifts, this apostle asked his hearers to imagine a body consisting only of an eye or an ear.

2. A watchman could identify this Old Testament warrior's approach from afar off because he drove like a maniac.

3. He said that before we attempt to correct the faults of others, we correct our own faults, which are like big logs lodged in our eyes.

4. When the Philistines captured the Ark of God and set it in their temple, they awoke to find that this idol had fallen over in a prostrate position in front of the Ark.

5. Because of her advanced age, the idea that she and her elderly husband could have a child together struck her so funny that she burst out laughing.

6. To amuse wedding guests, this Old Testament warrior posed a riddle: From an eater, something to eat; out of the strong, something sweet

7. God caused this man's donkey to speak to him, as he had allowed money to trump his own good sense.

8. When his daughter was raised from the dead, everyone was so astonished that they had to be reminded to get her something to eat.

9. When Peter escaped from prison and knocked on the door of his friends' home, the servant girl was so surprised to hear his voice that she failed to open the door and let him in.

a. Jesus

b. Sarah

c. Dagon

d. Rhoda

e. Paul

f. Balaam

g. Jehu

h. Samson

i. Jairus

Big Puzzler

Warning: Some are punny!

ACROSS

1 Disconnected
4 Male deer
9 Clammy
12 __ de Janeiro
13 Impressionist painter
14 Hearer
15 Computer keyboard key
16 Stadium
17 Exist
18 Bake shelled eggs
20 Yesterday's dimple
22 Airport abbr.
24 Time period
25 Ambassador's offices
29 Agreed (with)
33 Domestic help
34 Dawdle
36 Salute in Mexico City
37 Undo a knot
39 Tired, with "out"
41 I-dolatry
43 Sodom fleer
44 Sluggish one (archaic)
48 Cries
52 Excitement
53 31 Down grandson
55 By way of
56 M.D., for short
57 English tea go-with
58 Sick
59 __ of the Covenant
60 Perceive
61 Allow

DOWN

1 Mined metals
2 You find them in a school
3 Central points
4 Stings
5 Sticky black substance
6 Fresh
7 Style, as in music
8 They're always up to something
9 Flimsy
10 Banjo player Scruggs
11 Maple
19 Prepared
21 Innocence
23 Handy way to communicate
25 Flightless bird
26 Woman's partner
27 Fragment

DOWN CON'T

28 Talk
30 Org. head
31 Adam's wife
32 Male parent
35 It can make your hair stand on end
38 Exodus
40 Common finch
42 Kitchen measurement
44 Pop
45 Smell
46 It's all keyed up
47 Sky light
49 Wicked
50 Heap
51 It's useful in a pinch
54 Brain and spinal cord together (Abbr.)

WHY WAIT?

Waiting in line...waiting for Christmas, or summer, or vacation...waiting while forms are being processed, permission comes through, the acceptance letter arrives, we're finally given the go-ahead...waiting to see the face of a loved one after a long absence. Waiting for the decision, the news, the outcome. We spend a lot of time waiting!

Yet there's something we never need to wait for, and that's an opportunity to be a kind and loving person. Right now, you can consciously replace unpleasant or fearful thoughts with heart-warming, positive ones. The thoughts that bring a smile to your face. Wherever you are, you can mentally gather your blessings from near and far, and negative feelings disappear like shadows in sunlight. Your gratitude leaves no room for them!

When you're kind and loving on the inside, your "outside" can't help but follow. You'll want to speak gentle words, help out where needed, and share generously with others. You'll experience the joy and satisfaction of being able to trust, to contribute, to change things for the better. Ask yourself: Why wait?

Dear God, grant me the joy of being the kind of person You want me to be.

Kind and Loving

Throughout the Bible, there are many instances of people—people just like us—going out of their way to show kindness and love to others. Match the incident in the first column with the man or woman's name in the second column.

1. God put a mark on him that forbade anyone from murdering him, even though he was a murderer.

2. Priscilla and her husband, Aquila, helped this new believer preach the Gospel with increased knowledge and accuracy.

3. This evangelist opened the Scriptures, and baptized, a God-fearing man from Ethiopia.

4. She, wife of Chuza, was among many wealthy women who financially supported Jesus and His disciples.

5. This aunt of the child-prince Joash hid him and his nurse to protect him from her sister's intent to kill the young prince.

6. She rejoiced with Mary at the news of her pregnancy, and undoubtedly encouraged the young women during this time.

7. She and another woman arrived early in the morning at Jesus' tomb, intending to anoint His body.

8. Paul gave this would-be missionary another chance to prove himself after he had abandoned a previous trip.

9. He spared King Saul's life, even though he knew that Saul was plotting to kill him.

10. She begged the king to spare the life of her husband, Nabal, despite the fact the surly man had insulted the king's servants.

a. Philip

b. Mary Magdalene

c. Cain

d. David

e. Joanna

f. Apollos

g. Barnabas

h. Elizabeth

i. Jehosheba

j. Abigail

ANOTHER TRY

Years ago, you might have made an attempt that failed. But now is different. If it's still in your heart to accomplish, why not try again? This time, go about it in a different way. You have skills you didn't have before. Maybe better resources are available...maybe you'll see things you didn't notice the first time around.

If you have a hunch you can do it, give it a go. Sometimes a hunch is God's way of saying, "Now is the time."

Dear God, if now is the time, help me to try again.

Trying Words

It's always a good time to try these things!

ACROSS

- 2 Friendly
- 5 Fearless
- 7 Candid
- 9 Rely on
- 11 Aware
- 13 Dependable
- 14 Be concerned
- 16 Please
- 20 Constant
- 21 Exultant
- 22 Respectful
- 24 Zealous
- 27 Astute
- 28 Out-loud grin
- 31 Gentleness

DOWN

- 1 Smart
- 3 Belief in God
- 4 Nice
- 6 Thankfulness
- 8 Enduring
- 10 Grin
- 12 Satisfied
- 14 Level-headed
- 15 Lighthearted
- 17 Diplomatic

DOWN CON'T

18 Undertaking
19 Bravery
23 Affection
25 Aid
26 Generous
29 Look forward to, with "for"
30 Serenity

WEAKNESS TO STRENGTH

Who **among us** has never wished to have no **weaknesses**? No more **misspoken** words, hurtful remarks, mean-spirited thoughts, **embarrassing** gaffs, lost tempers, **wrongful** actions, or foolish **decisions**! Despite our **lofty ideals**, however, **each one** of us is forced to face the fact that we're far from **perfect**. Personal **shortcomings**, no matter how hard we try to avoid them, continue to play a part in our lives and in the lives of **everyone** else.

Our weaknesses never **please God**; nonetheless, He **turns them** around and uses them for **our good**. How could we ever receive His gift of a **humble heart**, except by fully **admitting** that we have **plenty to** be humble about? All we **need to do** is review what we have done and what we have **failed** to do. Why would we place **any value** on **forgiveness** if we thought we **didn't need it**? And if we didn't need forgiveness, we'd have little **incentive** to extend it to others. Without weaknesses to **overcome**, self-mastery would **elude us**. We'd never know the **satisfaction** of having overcome a weakness, nor would we have the ability **to help** others do so, too.

Most **importantly**, our weaknesses **invite us** to draw closer to God. He has the **power** and the **desire** to **transform** our personal weaknesses into God-given **strengths**.

Dear God, show me where You work
Your strength in my weaknesses.

Strong Words

Find the reading's **bolded** words in the word search puzzle.

```
I K Q S A N Y V A L U E O E V I T N E C N I
K G B U I M P O R T A N T L Y C Z H Q F W G
N L U L S Y M P O K B B L K D W W M R E E F
A I E O B M C A H E N O I T C A F S I T A S
D Z R F E D W X A K T Q D W H S G N E X K B
M V I T U E N O H C A E D H T W A V Q P N D
I Q S Y X A P O W E R J E R N W E T T K E E
T Y E I S Q M R Y F I L E E V R N O C C S L
T N D D H T M Z O Y U N E O Y M H F I O S B
I M Q E O M R Y X D G D J O N E Y S C V E H
N T B A R I X A E T T H N V L M I Y E E S V
G U U L T S W U H O L E I P T O V W O R S L
Y R S S C S S S D O H J O S N Y A D G C F U
Z N W G O P H O D Y R T C S S R S F K O N T
L S T W M O V S G L Y L M B N P G R B M S I
P T I F I K O J V T H F D V I N Z T E E J S
D H D F N E E J N I Q F R O I F R B R Y C S
P E E C G N T E U Y W M I S O A I D D B J E
D M E G S D L L H K R S S S E Z O V O L V N
H C N R O P I J Q O X A U H D G K D O U T E
I H T E K J P D F D R G E E E S V O G F C V
E P N P I P E S Y R N L Z S T A J C R G E I
S L D O P L N F A O B P A J C I F R U N F G
P W I O I A Z B M M V E T G F W V W O O R R
B W D A R O M A U N L B I X E C U N E R E O
H T F T H E W H I P P K K Q V F E Q I W P F
```

IMPERFECT BEAUTY

A chef strives for the perfect soufflé...a gardener to grow the perfect rose...an artist to create the perfect portrait...a teenager to meet the perfect person. We see great beauty in perfection.

Yet there's often even greater beauty in what isn't technically perfect, like a home-cooked meal that's a family favorite...a drooping dandelion clutched in a toddler's chubby hand...an expressive composition that speaks volumes...an "imperfect" face that accompanies a warm personality and loving heart.

Seeming perfection may garner the oooooh's and ahhhh's of an audience, but if you want to discover the kind of beauty that can touch your heart, explore the beauty of imperfect things...faces...people.

Dear God, as You value us despite our imperfections, teach me to value others.

Perfectly True

Follow the clues by crossing off words in the grid. Some words might be crossed off by more than one clue. When you are finished, the remaining words form a quotation by Ralph Waldo Emerson, reading down one column at a time.

1. Cross out names of capital cities.
2. Cross out names of books of the Bible.
3. Cross out articles of clothing.
4. Cross out things you might see in the sky.
5. Cross out names of trees, plants, and flowers.
6. Cross out words denoting size.
7. Cross out words denoting strength.
8. Cross out words that contain two of the letters R, S and T.

MIGHTY	CLOUDS	OR
BELT	BEAUTIFUL	FERN
THOUGH	DAISY	WE
PALM	WE	NOVA
WE	HUGE	MOON
ROME	GREAT	FIND
STARS	WASHINGTON	POTENT
TRAVEL	MUST	TICKETS
SEAS	POWERFUL	IT
THE	CARRY	DRESS
WORLD	MARK	OVER
ROBE	PARIS	LILY
OAK	IT	GIGANTIC
TO	MADRID	STREAMS
NUMBERS	WITH	NOT
FIND	ACTS	GRATITUDE
THE	ROSE	
RIVER	US	

Saying: _____

COMPASSION IN ACTION

During His ministry on Earth, Jesus taught many of His lessons through parables—stories we can readily understand. They deal with shepherds and their sheep, farmers and their land, women and their home, families and their struggles. Jesus' parables are more than simple stories, because each one has a spiritual meaning.

Take, for example, His well-known parable about the Lost Son. In this story, the younger of two sons asks for—and receives—his inheritance from his father. This son leaves home and soon squanders all the money he had, ending up in abject poverty. He starts to think about the home he left, comforts he enjoyed, and the place he once possessed in a stable and loving family. So he decides to return to his father, confess his irrationality, and hope his father might let him stay on as a servant.

But before this son even reaches the doorstep of his home, his father—who had been waiting for his son's return—ran out to meet him. This compassionate father threw his arms around his son, welcomed him back, and restored to him all the privileges of a beloved son.

No matter where you are spiritually—or physically—God's arms are open. You are His, and you are always welcome back...from any place, at any time.

Dear God, thank You for Your never-changing compassion.

Great Stories!

Jesus parables have been defined as earthly stories with heavenly meanings. Match the "earthly story" in the first column with the "heavenly meaning" in the second column.

1. A farmer sows seed in many kinds of soil; some seeds take root, and others do not.

2. A widow pleas for justice; she finally receives it, because the judge realizes she will not give up.

3. A Samaritan who was looked down upon was the only one who stopped to help a man in need.

4. A shepherd discovers that one sheep has wandered away; he leaves to search for it.

5. One man built his house on sand, and it fell; another built on rock, and it withstood the storm.

6. It's an ill-advised builder who starts building before he knows if he's able to complete it!

7. A manager erased his servant's debt, but the servant demanded payment from those owing him.

8. Three servants received money; two invested it and reaped a profit; the third simply returned it.

9. Workers were all paid the same, whether they worked all day or only part of the day.

a. The one we despise may possess more faith, compassion, and generosity than we do.

b. We are to fully use whatever gifts God give us and not let them lie dormant.

c. Firm faith in God will carry us through life's troubles and difficulties.

d. God rewards persistence in prayer; at the right time, He will answer.

e. Discipleship may cost us, and we should know this before we declare ourselves His disciples.

f. Because God forgives us, we must forgive others.

g. God is as generous to new believers as He is to life-long believers.

h. Some who receive God's Word believe; others reject the gift of faith.

i. God will not fail to notice if even one of us strays from faith in Him; and He will look for us.

LIFE FULFILLMENT

Children, career, profession, knowledge, talent, skill, experience, social status...all these gains enrich our lives.

Lasting fulfillment, however, comes from what we give. Our help, friendship, encouragement are all things meant to be given away. We can share our talents...our time...our caring. We can pray for others.

Life enrichment is all about what you receive...but life fulfillment is all about what you give.

Dear God, teach me to give freely and generously to others.

The Giving Life

There are countless ways to give—this puzzle includes some of them!

ACROSS

1 Uphold
3 Counsel
5 Pardon
6 Improve
11 Divide
14 Togetherness
16 Hear
17 Go ahead of
18 Goodwill
21 Instruct
24 Act compassionately (2 words)
25 Put others __: be magnanimous
26 Pat on __: congratulate (2 words)
27 Go __ for: act on behalf of another (2 words)
28 Cure

DOWN

2 Esteem
4 Contribute with no charge

DOWN CON'T

7 Speak to God on behalf of (2 words)
8 Encourage
9 Construct
10 Direct
12 Respite
13 Compliment
15 Help out (3 words)
19 Thoughtfulness
20 Nourish
22 Soothe
23 Spur on
24 A benediction
26 Spend __ with: visit

🌸 GENUINE INTEREST

Have you ever talked with someone who's passionate about his or her hobby or pastime? You don't need to prod them for interesting stories on the topic, and you're likely to come away with delightful tidbits of information that you would have never guessed. In all likelihood, you'll pass on your newfound knowledge to your friends the next time you get together. Then again, maybe you'll be so intrigued that you'll consider taking up the activity yourself.

While it's fun to dabble here and there at various things that strike our fancy, it's far more rewarding to passionately pursue a singular, heartfelt interest. Focusing on one activity or body of knowledge keeps us engaged with life, broadens our horizons, heightens our creativity and imagination, builds our skills…and most of all, sparks lively conversations and creates lasting friendships.

If you already have a hobby you love, give thanks for the blessing—because it is a blessing. Savor the joy it brings to your life, and think of ways your special interest might benefit others, or inspire them to pursue their own passion. If you have yet to get started, what's keeping you? Even a little time spent following your heart is time well spent.

Thank You, dear God, for giving me the gift of special interests.

The Giving Life

In the list on the next page, find the answer to each clue.

ORNITHOLOGIST   BIBLIOPHILE
GEOCACHER   RAPPELLER
GENEALOGIST   APIARIST
PHILATELIST   DELTIOLOGIST
NUMISMATIST   AUDIOPHILE
CRYPTOLOGIST   CALLIGRAPHER

1. Stamp collector: _____

2. Ancestry seeker: _____

3. Code breaker: _____

4. Coin collector: _____

5. Lettering artist: _____

6. Bird observer: _____

7. Beekeeper: _____

8. GPS-armed searcher: _____

9. Cliff descender: _____

10. Book collector: _____

11. Postcard collector: _____

12. Music enthusiast: _____

SWINGING TIME

See the pendulum of a cuckoo clock—it swings right to left, left to right. Its constant back-and-forth motion illustrates the way many of us view ourselves. One moment we're on top of the world. We feel savvy, powerful, and full of potential. The next moment we're completely down on ourselves. We tally our mistakes and missteps, and decide there's nothing left to hope for. And then the whole cycle repeats itself.

Neither extreme reflects the truth. Both fantasies are common, and they spring from an exaggerated sense of importance on one side, and feelings of helplessness on the other. An objective look, however, places us right alongside our neighbor. Not one of us is better than another. No one is loved by God more or less than anyone else. As Augustine so aptly said, "God loves each of us as if there were only one of us."

At the same time, not one of us is of less worth than our neighbor. Each of us possesses life, a gift from God, and a soul that is priceless. We may stumble and we may fail; we may triumph and succeed; but God's love—and our value—never changes.

Keep the pendulum going on the cuckoo clock—but put a stop to it in your heart and mind!

Dear God, help me maintain a balanced view of myself.

Two Sides

Put the answer to Clue 1 in box 1. Scramble the letters and drop one letter to answer Clue 2. Write the word in box 2 and the dropped letter in the left-hand box. Scramble the letters and drop one letter to answer Clue 3. Write the word in box 3 and the dropped letter in the right-hand box. Complete each row the same way, starting with a new word. When you're finished, reading vertically on the left, you'll find the name of a disciple who sinned and lost all hope; and on the right, a disciple who sinned, but asked for and received forgiveness.

1. He had a coat of many colors
2. Expects
3. Footwear
4. Uses a blender
5. Shopping __: wild spending
6. Agents, for short
7. Became anxious
8. Most high schoolers
9. Observed
10. Cognizant
11. Pottery, for example
12. Not cooked
13. Declare
14. Ogle
15. Fill up

	1.	2.	3.	
	4.	5.	6.	
	7.	8.	9.	
	10.	11.	12.	
	13.	14.	15.	

139

Big Puzzler

We hope this is neither extremely hard nor extremely easy, but just right!

ACROSS

1 Rug type
5 Flow's partner
8 Took a chair
11 Upkeep
12 Pod dweller
13 Canal
14 Baker's need
15 Spots
16 Zilch
17 Letter styles
19 Put down
21 Ag. org.
22 King David's composition
24 Obtained
27 Bongo, for one
28 Tending (to)
30 Unkind person
33 Tested
34 City area
35 Baby's bed
36 Mr.'s partner
37 Claw
39 ___ chi
42 Norway's capital
43 Small branches
45 Short form, for short
48 Ship letters
50 Cain's brother
51 Light need
52 Lion name
53 Garden creeper
54 Omaha summer hour
55 Sum up
56 Has lunch

DOWN

1 Tease
2 Chaos
3 Playing field
4 Polite man, for short
5 Climate org.
6 Confusion
7 Elemental
8 Madrid Mrs.
9 Help
10 Beverage
13 Conclusion
18 Dashes
20 Etch in
23 Take to court
24 State official, for short

DOWN CON'T

25 Only
26 Commandment number
27 Genetic code letters
29 Steal
30 Silent
31 Sin
32 Body builder's pride, for short
33 For
35 Shut
38 Birds "thumb"
39 Leg bone
40 Representative
41 Oahu and others
42 Ball
44 Wordless "hi"
45 Pre-K letters
46 Develop
47 Deli order, for short
49 Turf

THE GOOD FIGHT

Half-baked opinions...silly propositions...unknowable answers...self-serving pride. You can let go of all those things! All they do is waste your time and get you mired in a tangle of empty words and unproductive ideas.

Truth...justice and fairness...honesty...meaningful relationships...compassion and kindness...personal well-being. Now those things are worth fighting for! While you may love peace and would prefer peace to confrontation, you demean yourself if you simply sit back and allow others to, say, take undue advantage of you, tell lies about you, or willfully put you or others in danger.

More? Becoming your best self is worth fighting for, and it's a lifelong struggle for everyone. But if you take the easy route and rest on your laurels, you stop growing, maturing, and savoring the joy of life. Defending your rights and the rights of others warrants your commitment, no matter the cost. Speaking out for what's good and God-pleasing is worth the wounds of ridicule that could come your way.

Just as in any battle, there's no guarantee that you'll personally see victory. But if you persevere, you're sure to receive the satisfaction of proving that you stand for positive, uplifting values—the kind of values that always seem to win in the end.

Dear God, help me let go of small annoyances,
but meet the challenge of things worth fighting for.

The Battle Won

With God's help, each of these Bible figures bravely confronted their enemies. Choose the right answer for each clue.

1. This Israelite captive in Babylon, along with two others, risked perishing in a fiery furnace rather than bow down to the idol that King Nebuchadnezzar had set up.
   a. Meshach
   b. Daniel
   c. Haman

2. By asking the king for a favor, this Israelite queen put her life on the line for the sake of her people.
   a. Esther
   b. Sheba
   c. Deborah

3. This early believer prophesied that the apostle Paul would be arrested if we went to Jerusalem; Paul replied that even if it meant death, he would proceed to Jerusalem and spread the Gospel message.
   a. Priscilla
   b. Philip
   c. Agabus

4. King Herod had this early-church leader put to death so he could win the approval of temple leaders who did not accept Jesus Christ.
   a. Peter
   b. James
   c. Silas

5. This disciple suffered many trials and was finally exiled to the island of Patmos on account of his faithfulness to the Gospel message.
   a. John
   b. Andrew
   c. Philip

6. According to tradition, this disciple was crucified upside down by the Emperor Nero.
   a. James
   b. Peter
   c. John

7. His wife chided him for remaining faithful to God, even though he had suffered grievous loss.
   a. Jeremiah
   b. Ezekiel
   c. Job

8. A riot broke out in this city when the apostle Paul proclaimed the Gospel, angering silversmiths who made a good living selling images of idols.
   a. Corinth
   b. Ephesus
   c. Berea

GOOD PLAN

Some say, "Play it safe." Others will tell you, "Go for it!" As so often is the case, however, the wisest choice lies somewhere in between.

Foolhardy risks and impulsive decisions rarely benefit anyone; in fact, lifelong consequences most often follow in their wake. On the other hand, if we're afraid to ever take one step beyond our comfort zone, or fear to go where the outcome is uncertain, we rob ourselves of opportunities for experience, exploration, discovery, and achievement. Many great things have happened because someone was brave enough to act on an outside-the-box idea. Many lives have been enhanced and uplifted because someone took a chance on an unexpected desire.

When you consider something you would like to do, take time to examine your course of action. If it's a sound plan, it will withstand the test of time...it will hold up to scrutiny...it will prove strong enough to weather the questions and criticisms of others without becoming defensive or angry. Like a loyal friend, it will stick with you. Like a genuine, heartfelt urging, you will come to realize that this is the right thing for you to do.

Dear God, help me discern when to play it safe and when to go ahead.

Chance Taken

Many Bible figures took a chance without being certain of the outcome. Match the name in the first column with the chance he or she took in the second column.

1. Jacob	a. He took a chance that, despite God's startling orders to sacrifice his only son, there would be an heir, as God had promised.
2. Noah	b. He took a chance that Jesus would heal his servant, even though he was a gentile.
3. Ruth	c. It must have appeared bizarre to see a man build a boat where there was no water, but this man took a chance and obeyed God's instructions.
4. Abraham	d. When Eli the priest said that God would answer her prayer, she went home content and comforted.
5. Ananias	e. Had his brother changed his mind after all these years, or did he still want to kill him? He took a chance that his brother had changed.
6. Miriam	f. Jesus said, "Come," and he stepped out of the boat and onto the water of the Sea of Galilee.
7. Centurion	g. She took a chance by remaining with her mother-in-law; after all, she'd be a foreigner, and perhaps no one would accept her.
8. Peter	h. When God told him to meet with Paul, a known persecutor of Christians at that time, he took a chance that Paul would not arrest him.
9. Hannah	i. When her baby brother was left near Pharaoh's palace, she watched, taking a chance that the infant would be taken in and cared for.

OPPORTUNITY KNOCKS

Have you ever thought about where you'd like to be five, ten, or fifteen years from now? Perhaps you've created a detailed plan of action designed to take you from place to place in a specific span of time. Or maybe you have only a vague idea of what you'd like to be doing in the coming years, rarely giving it much thought.

Either way, here's something to consider. Only God knows what the future holds, and we sometimes pass up the opportunities He puts in front of us. Why? Because for some of us, the God-sent opportunity doesn't fit our plans, so we ignore it. Looking back, we realize what we've missed! For others among us, the God-sent opportunity comes unexpectedly, but we'd rather continue doing what's comfortable and familiar than take it. Later, all we can do is sigh, "I wish I had!"

God may use the chances, changes, connections, and coincidences of today to bless your tomorrow. Who knows what the future will bring? God does!

*Dear God, lead me on Your path today
and through all my tomorrows.*

Plan for Today

Find synonyms for contentment as you unscramble these letters. When you are finished, unscramble the letters in parenthesis for another word of contentment!

1. Y E T E R I N S

   (_) _ _ _ _ _ _ _

2. C O A T S I N A F I S T

   _ _ _ _ _ _ _ _ (_) _ _ _ _

3. R E U S E L A P

   _ _ _ _ _ (_) _ _ _ _

4. T O Y J E M E N N

   _ _ _ _ _ _ _ (_) _ _

5. L I F T U N L F L E M

   _ (_) _ _ _ _ _ _ _ _ _

6. E V E N T H E M I C A

   _ (_) _ _ _ _ _ _ _ _ _

7. G I N T H I S

   _ _ (_) _ _ _ _ _

   Answer: _ _ _ _ _ _ _

YOU CAN CHANGE

Few of us would **claim** that there's *nothing* about our lives that we'd like to **change**, or at least **adjust** in **some way**. Maybe **improved** health...**additional** money in the bank **account**...a new **wardrobe**, car, or home...a **family** member, friend, or **coworker** who would not make unkind **remarks** and critical comments... more time to do the things we would **like to do**...more **hours** in the day.

But not **everything** is changeable, **at least** not by us. Though we make the best **decisions** we can, use our resources **wisely**, and strive to **influence** the **behavior** of others, there are things we don't have the power to **alter**. Some circumstances are completely out of our **control**, and other people—even those **closest** to us—ultimately are **responsible** for their own **choices**.

What you have the **God-given** power to **transform**, however, is **yourself**. A can-do mindset motivates you **to take** on those things that you're able to **affect** in a **positive** way. A **perceptive** mind tells you what lies **beyond** your control, and **trust in God** allows you to let it go and let Him **handle** it. A light **heart** gives you everything you need to remain **joyful** and **confident** through it all!

Grant me the ability, dear God, to know my strengths...
and my limitations.

Full Control

Find the reading's **bolded** words in the word search puzzle.

```
J O Y F U L O F L E S R U O Y E Z Q F K W T
S A T P S K W H T S O M E W A Y I A D F R G
D R G G S O S G N I H T O N M N W K J U T A
L N L E B M V D I P P H F Q F J J M S L T C
O M N A X U F T I D I Z W L E A R T B L O G
U E B O R D R A W O J B U V C Y I B E N O H
Z R O I V A H E B Q F E E C O N H A T D E K
U E K Z W I S E L Y N R O B G D S R G A I Q
X G K C W Z L I K C Y U D O P T O I R C H M
C N T S Y Q L Y E T N I D T S L V T B C S J
X A F O S A B D H T A J L W E E T F E O I F
M H Q E T B X I C T Z S A A N V M C M K A A
F C C Q W A N W Z E U P V P N L I I E M I E
L R H P C G K S V A S E E N G O A T I F H L
Z T R A S C O E K J E O J R R L I L I O F I
D S E E N N J B K W C E U T C E Y T C S K A
I E T L X D O E K H I X Q W N E K M I J O K
M S L B I O L I H W O M K M Y E P R P D B P
P O A I A N J E S Q H L R V R S D T O K D D
R L J S F Y Q C R I C Z A I K O K I I W O A
O C R N L R E E T S C Z B L O D F R F V O P
V M R O S Y H J P S A E O K N T K S A N E C
E P W P S R Y J O E U Z D O L P E D N M O B
D Y G S K I U V S P M J Y N T W O J M A E C
S F N E P W V O V X V E D V N Q V X G S R R
K C O R H Q X J H V B O K A Z Q L L Z M V T
```

IT SHOWS

Your relationship with God shows in the way you live. Confident living shows you lean on God for strength...worry-free living shows you trust Him with your problems...secure living shows you rely on Him to guide you...thankful living shows you know He's the source of every blessing...joyful living shows—really shows!—in your relationship with others.

Even when you aren't saying a word, God shows in you!

Dear God, let Your love shine through me!

Show Me!

Many figures in the Bible said, "Show me!" You'll find a few of them in this puzzle.

ACROSS

1 Competent
5 Land measurement
9 Where Jesus' showed His sacrifice
11 Old Testament idol
12 Bog
13 Caribbean nation
14 Abort
15 Portland locale (Abbr.)
17 "Show me my offense and my __" (Job 13:23 niv)
18 Made coffee
20 Grass cutting blade
22 Pronoun for Mary or Martha
23 Southern African nation (Abbr.)
24 Caesarea to Nazareth dir.
27 "The __ and the lamb shall feed together" (Isa. 65:25)
29 Loot
31 Sheaf
32 What Jesus showed Thomas, who doubted His resurrection
33 "The Lord is __ to anger" (Nah. 1:3)
34 Jesus __ from the tomb

DOWN

1. Peak
2. Cereal choice
3. "Show me your ways, __, teach me your paths" (Psa. 25:4 niv)
4. Kind of curve
5. First letters
6. Motive
7. Ill rodent, maybe
8. Dash
10. Summer clothing
16. Bring up again
18. "He shall be like a tree planted __ the rivers" (Psa. 1:3)
19. "Forgive us our debts, as __ forgive our debtors" (Matt. 6:12)
20. Shallow area in a river
21. Large stringed instrument
22. Compass point
24. Taboo (2 words)
25. Offers
26. Otherwise
28. "Harvest truly is plenteous, but the laborers are __" (Matt. 9:37)
30. Golfer's goal

PEACE WITHIN

Who among us would knowingly and willingly carry around a bundle of thorns on our back? With every step we take during the day—ouch! We long to sleep at night, but can't get comfortable because we're lying on a bed of spikes. The pain and discomfort is 24/7!

That's what we're doing to ourselves when we let bitterness take over heart and mind. There's no place we can go that we're not reminded of what happened...of our feelings, our loss, our wounds... of the consequences we've had to endure...and most particularly, of who's responsible. Yet remaining bitter only adds to our misery. It has no power to change the facts. It's unable to soothe, heal, or comfort. It punishes no one except ourselves.

When you choose to forgive, you are doing yourself a favor. Your forgiveness never lessens the enormity of the offense, or implies that the person who committed it shouldn't be brought to justice. Simply put, heart-deep forgiveness means that you are not going to let someone else's sin define your life. You are going to seek strength, healing, and peace...and the only place you will find it is in forgiveness.

Dear God, grant me the strength and the willingness to forgive.

Transformations

Change the first word into the second word of each pair by replacing only one letter at a time. Do not scramble letter order; use only common English words, and no capitalized words.

Example:

   LOSE
   lone
   line
   fine
   FIND

1. HARD

_____
_____
_____
_____
_____

SOFT

2. MEAN

_____
_____
_____
_____
_____

KIND

3. HATE

_____
_____
_____
_____
_____

PITY

4. COLD

_____
_____
_____
_____
_____

WARM

5. PAIN

_____
_____
_____
_____
_____

HEAL

WHAT'S FOR DINNER?

It's said that "you are what you eat." While you might not describe yourself in terms of what you had for dinner last night, the expression highlights the importance of good food to your body. When you make healthy, tasty, wholesome choices, you not only find pleasure in eating, but provide nourishment your body can use. Your appearance, energy level, and present and future health are directly connected to the food you eat.

Your spiritual health, too, depends on what you "feed" your heart and soul. A steady diet of sound teaching, prayerful reading, serious thinking, and humble acceptance of God's Word and His will is sure to keep you in tip-top spiritual shape!

Dear God, show me how to fill both body and soul with good, nourishing foods.

Bible Foods

Nourishing food was as important, and as necessary, in Bible times as it is today. Use the Bible "grocery list" to complete the puzzle grid; one word has been filled in to get you started.

FOUR LETTERS

CORN	LAMB
EGGS	MILK
FIGS	MINT
FISH	NUTS
	SALT

FIVE LETTERS

BEANS
CUMIN
HONEY
LEEKS
WHEAT

SIX LETTERS

BARLEY GRAPES
BUTTER MELONS
CHEESE OLIVES
GARLIC ONIONS

SEVEN LETTERS

ALMONDS
LENTILS
MUSTARD
VENISON

FISH

LOVE IN ACTION

There are many different kinds of love. The term includes love of spouse, children, relatives, friends, colleagues, coworkers, neighbors, fellow church members, strangers, and people of other places and cultures. Yet genuine love, no matter what kind or for whom, compels us to express it in practical, self-giving actions.

Without observable action, our words of love are meaningless... our feelings of love have no substance. And if our actions come only when it's easy and convenient for us, or when they coincide with our personal preferences, clearly love-of-self overrides love-of-other.

In the Bible's often-quoted "Love is" chapter (1 Corinthians 13), the apostle Paul describes love in terms of action. Love is kind and patient, respectful and gentle, generous and slow to take offense. True love puts others first and considers their needs and well-being, even going out of its way to do so. Love doesn't entertain mean thoughts, or utter unhelpful and unnecessary criticisms, or willfully harm anyone. Genuine love can't help but result in constant, daily, God-pleasing, and visible actions...simply because that's the way love is.

How will you show "I love you" today?

Dear God, thank You for all the ways you show You love me; help me extend love-in-action to others.

Love Is

Each clue suggests a loving action or characteristic. Within the answer word, there is a word that corresponds to the bolded clue-element.

Example:
Large hibernating mammal's self-control: FOR**BEAR**ANCE

1. Empathy for a **direction-determining device**:

   _ _ _ _ _ _ _ _ _ _

2. **Serenade** of good fortune:

   _ _ _ _ _ _ _ _

3. Determination not to **disunite**:

   _ _ _ _ _ _ _ _ _ _ _

4. Is generous with a **writing instrument**:

   _ _ _ _ _ _ _ _ _

5. A suitable **item for a stage play**:

   _ _ _ _ _ _ _ _ _ _

6. Friendly **TV channel-provider**:

   _ _ _ _ _ _ _ _

7. Not given to boasting in a **canvas shelter**:

   _ _ _ _ _ _ _ _ _ _ _ _

8. **Relating to us**, it's only polite:

   _ _ _ _ _ _ _ _ _

9. Caring **adjacency**:

   _ _ _ _ _ _ _ _ _ _

10. Helpful **harbor for cruise ships**:

    _ _ _ _ _ _ _ _

157

ONCE UPON A TIME

Have you ever attended a class reunion? Perhaps the first thing you noticed was how much some of your former classmates have changed. Although physical appearance is the most noticeable, there's more than meets the eye. The important changes are the ones you discover only after you venture beyond "hello."

Gone is the silliness of the former class clown...the arrogance of the privileged few...the overconfidence of the person voted most likely to succeed. They have deepened, matured, and mellowed. Rumors, rivalries, appraisals, and comparisons melt away as you chat with the former directionless classmate who found his niche in life...the materialistic one who now supports charitable foundations...the mean-spirited one whose life experiences opened her eyes to love and compassion...the quiet one who leads the reunion committee and welcomes everyone with warmth and confidence.

Once upon a time, we were all children. We may have been unfairly labeled; or correctly characterized based on our behavior then. But the years have brought us more than simply grown-up bodies. We have the gift of being able to change in all the best and truest ways.

Dear God, let me celebrate the positive changes people have made in their lives, and the ones I have made in mine.

How They Changed!

God worked big changes in the lives of Bible figures, just as He does in the lives of people today. Match the names in the first column with the change God produced in them in the second column.

1. Abraham — a. Rural sheepherder and fig farmer turned preacher to the Samaritans, urging morality and righteousness.

2. Paul — b. Hebrew raised in luxury of Pharaoh's household turned sheepherder and later, leader of Israelites.

3. Esther — c. Wealthy, settled landowner in Ur turned nomad as he gathers his household and sets out for Canaan.

4. Deborah — d. Pious but immature youth turned outspoken, fiery preacher urging a return to God's laws and worship of Him alone.

5. Moses — e. Moabite girl turned believer in the God of Israel and great-grandmother of King David.

6. Jeremiah — f. Intellectually gifted and classically trained Pharisee turned Christian believer and tireless missionary.

7. Amos — g. Israelite judge who settled disputes between people turned courageous and victorious military leader.

8. Ruth — h. Socially scorned sinner turned forgiven, redeemed, and highly esteemed disciple of Jesus.

9. Mary Magdalene — i. Beautiful and faithful Jewish girl turned wife of King Ahasuerus and queen of Persia.

ANSWERED PRAYER

Most of us can think of times when we were glad we didn't get what we had prayed for. Thank God—and we do!—He cares about us so much that He will tell us "No" whenever necessary.

God has no problem saying "Yes," either. His "Yes" may come exactly as we expected, but often His "Yes" appears quite different. We don't see it because it's not what we were looking for. If we're willing to look, however, we'll realize His "Yes" is far better than we could ever have imagined.

Dear God, open my eyes so I may see the many blessings You have given me.

Good, Better, Best

This puzzle is full of fun things!

ACROSS

1. Doggy door
5. Flyer
9. Volcanic rock
10. Roof panel, perhaps
11. Guitarist Clapton
12. Strong thread
13. Guidance
15. Wanted poster letters
16. Liberty
18. Conversations with God
21. Med. test
22. Sports team
26. In a tilted position
28. Good expectation
29. Little Miss Muffet's meal
30. Paradise
31. Historical time periods
32. Lease

DOWN

1. Pest
2. Shortening
3. Tel __
4. Soothe
5. Arrow launcher
6. Homeric saga
7. "Adventures of Tintin" ape
8. Imagine
10. Is at the helm
14. Old staircase sounds
17. Old Testament queen
18. Amity
19. Happen again
20. Ancient Greek marketplace
23. Traveled by car
24. What you do with a gift
25. Delivered by post
27. Jewel case contents, for short

SANCTUARY

Perhaps it's a whole room, or a comfy chair in the corner of a room...a shady spot in your garden or a window ledge lined with pots of herbs or flowers you have planted...an entire house, or a cabinet of your prized possessions. No matter how big or how small, it brings you a sense of peace and calmness. It is your personal sanctuary.

Call your sanctuary to mind. Name the items that make it special and meaningful. Find the words to describe colors, textures, and fragrance associated with it. Recall the feeling you have when you are there. As you think about your sanctuary, are there things you can do to heighten your pleasure in it? Make it more your own by adding something you love, or taking away something that detracts? Rearrange, neaten, or put things in order to further enhance the peace it offers?

Your sanctuary provides you a space apart from the daily routine, the demands of others, and the chaos of the world around you. It is in its presence that you gain strength, quietness, and peace of mind to carry with you wherever you go.

Dear God, let my heart find its true and lasting sanctuary in You.

Rhyme Time

Each clue can be answered with two rhyming words.

Example:
Optimist's question to moaner: **W H Y   S I G H?**

1. Sanctuary for Poe's bird:

_ _ _ _ _   _ _ _ _ _

2. Rent tranquility:

_ _ _ _ _   _ _ _ _ _

3. Blessing spot:

_ _ _ _ _   _ _ _ _ _ _

4. More elevated longing:

_ _ _ _ _ _   _ _ _ _ _ _ _

5. Discovered garden spot:

_ _ _ _ _   _ _ _ _ _ _

6. Grab time away:

_ _ _ _   _ _ _ _ _ _

7. A search for respite:

_ _ _ _   _ _ _ _ _ _

8. Reduced tension:

_ _ _ _   _ _ _ _ _ _ _

9. Attract amazement:

_ _ _ _   _ _ _

10. Sense authenticity:

_ _ _ _   _ _ _ _

🌟 FINDING THE GOLD

They say that silence is golden—but there are times when it isn't. Voices of peacemakers and truth-tellers, dispute-diffusers, information seekers, and levelheaded thinkers need to be heard, loud and clear! Probably in more instances than you realize, that voice is yours.

If you have a question, you'll never get an answer unless you ask it. If you feel passionately about something that concerns your well-being or the well-being of others, no one can know or take it seriously unless you articulate it. When you discover that justice isn't being served...truth isn't being told in its entirety...helpful criticism, necessary advice, a word of warning hasn't been uttered...other ideas and perspectives haven't been put forward...nothing will change until someone speaks up.

Each one of us is connected with others in families, friendships, associations, churches, groups, neighborhoods, and communities. Our involvement benefits everyone, and our participation serves to make our relationships stronger, more vibrant, and more meaningful.

Yes, there are times when silence is golden, because that's the only way you can listen. And there are times when what's golden is being heard.

Dear God, help me know when to remain silent and when to speak up.

Who Said It?

For each Bible quote, pick the right speaker and circumstance from the choices given.

1. "I know that my redeemer liveth."
   a. Jonah in the belly of a fish
   b. Job in the midst of misery
   c. Mary Magdalene at the open tomb

2. "Blessed are the peacemakers: for they shall be called the children of God."
   a. Jesus in the Sermon on the Mount
   b. King David as he declared victory over his foes.
   c. The apostle Paul as he urged believers to settle disputes.

3. "Come and see."
   a. Caleb when he reported back to Moses about the Promised Land.
   b. Philip-when Nathanael sneered at anything good coming out of Nazareth.
   c. Eve to Adam when she saw how pleasant the forbidden fruit appeared.

4. "Lord, I have heard by many of this man, how much evil he hath done to thy saints at Jerusalem."
   a. Hezekiah after reading Sennacherib's taunting letter.
   b. Joseph praying about King Herod's murderous threats.
   c. Ananias upon being asked to visit Saul of Tarsus.

5. "Against thee, sinned, and d sight."
   a. King David co of adultery and
   b. A Roman soldie the cross.
   c. Apostle Paul after his conversion, repenting his persecution of Christians.

6. "Lord, now lettest thou thy servant depart in peace, according to thy word."
   a. Moses' confession of faith as he breathed his last.
   b. Simeon's proclamation when he saw the infant Jesus.
   c. The frail apostle John's prayer of acceptance when he was in exile on Patmos.

7. "I advise you: Leave these men alone! ... For if their purpose or activity is of human origin, it will fail. But if it is from God, you will not be able to stop these men."
   a. The Pharisee Gamaliel addressing the Sanhedrin council concerning the apostles' teaching.
   b. Roman captain of the guard trying to calm the crowd demanding the arrest of Paul and Silas.
   c. Believer Aquila's defense of the disciples who had come to spread the gospel message in Corinth.

6/7

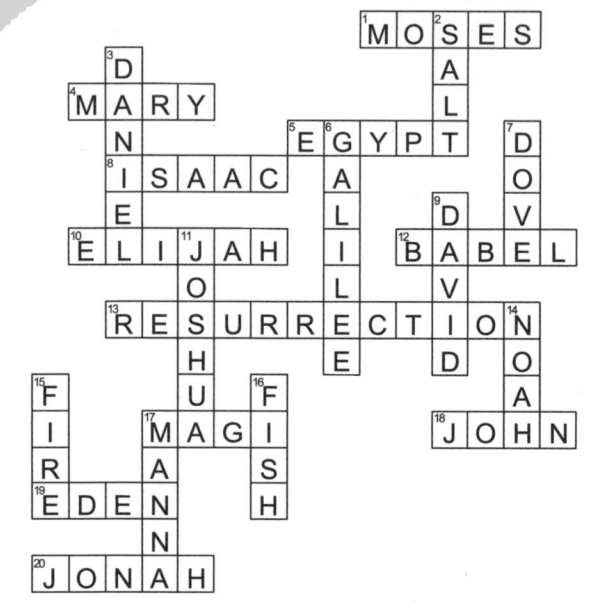

Crossword 1

Across: 1 MOSES, 4 MARY, 5 EGYPT, 8 ISAAC, 10 ELIJAH, 12 BABEL, 13 RESURRECTION, 18 JOHN, 19 EDEN, 20 JONAH, 17 MAGI

Down: 2 SALT, 3 DANIEL, 6 GALILEE, 7 DOVE, 9 DAVID, 11 JOHO(?), 14 NOAH(?), 15 FIRE, 16 FISH, 17 MANNA

PAGE 8/9

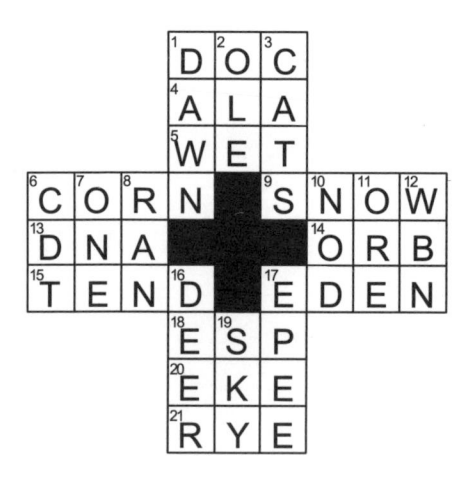

Across: 1 DOC, 4 ALA, 5 WET, 6 CORN, 9 SNOW, 13 DNA, 14 ORB, 15 TEND, 17 EDEN, 18 ESP, 20 EKE, 21 RYE

PAGE 10/11

1. False. Jesus said, "I am the way, the truth, and the life: no man cometh unto the Father, but by me" (John 14:6).
2. True. "Every house is builded by some man; but he that built all things is God" (Hebrews 3:4).
3. True. "In my Father's house are many mansions: if it were not so, I would have told you. I go to prepare a place for you" (John 14:2).
4. False. "If your brother or sister sins, go and point out their fault, just between the two of you. If they listen to you, you have won them over" (Matthew 18:15 NIV).
5. False. "If you, Lord, kept a record of sins, Lord, who could stand? But with you there is forgiveness" (Psalm 130:3-4 NIV).
6. False. "Forgive, and ye shall be forgiven" (Luke 6:37).
7. False. "If ye love me, keep my commandments" (John 14:15).
8. True. "The fruit of the Spirit is love, joy, peace, forbearance, kindness, goodness, faithfulness, gentleness and self-control" (Galatians 5:22-23 NIV).
9. False. "If thine enemy hunger, feed him; if he thirst, give him drink" (Romans 12:20).
10. True. "Let the word of Christ dwell in your richly" (Colossians 3:16).
11. True. "With God nothing shall be impossible" (Luke 1:37).

ANSWERS

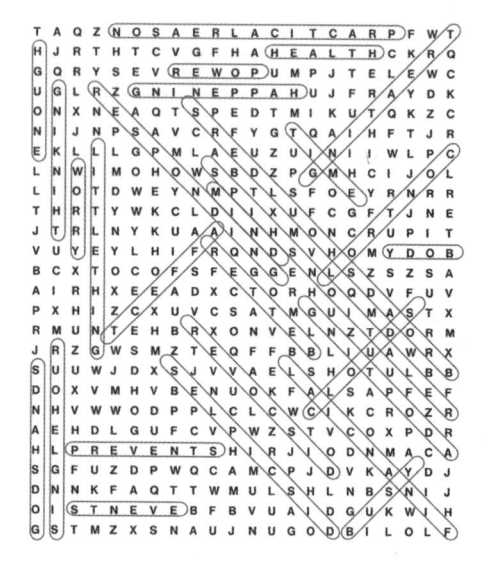

PAGE 12/13

PAGE 14/15

Saying: Two things are bad for the heart—running upstairs and running down people.

PAGE 16/17

T	A	B		R	A	G	E		C	A	L
A	W	E		A	G	E	S		T	A	X	I
L	O	T		B	R	A	T		H	U	L	K
C	L	A	B	B	E	R		T	U	T	E	E
		L	I	E		M	A	G	I			
A	L	E	U	T		S	A	D		O	A	F
L	O	V	E		J	O	Y		J	U	N	E
T	B	A		T	U	X		Z	E	S	T	Y
		L	O	N	G		S	O	S			
T	R	U	S	T		C	O	N	T	E	N	T
Z	E	A	L		S	A	R	I		S	A	A
A	L	T	O		O	P	E	N		P	V	C
R	Y	E			B	E	R	G		N	E	T

PAGE 18/19

Possible solutions:

1. TINY
tine
vine
vane
vase
VAST

2. POOR
pool
poll
pole
pile
rile
rice
RICH

3. LESS
loss
lose
lore
MORE

4. MEAN
mead
mend
mind
KIND

5. HOLD
hole
pole
pale
pave
gave
GIVE

PAGE 20/21

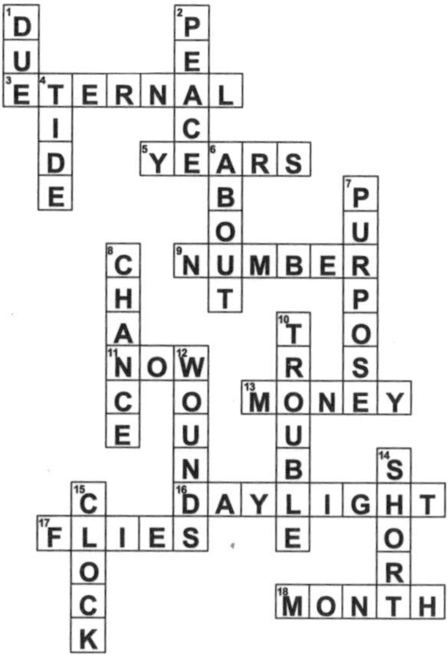
1 DUE
2 PEACE
3 ETERNAL
4 TIDE
5 YEARS
6 ABOUT
7 PURPOSE
8 CHANCE
9 NUMBER
10 TROUBLE
11 NOW
12 WOUNDS
13 MONEY
14 SHORT
15 CLOCK
16 DAYLIGHT
17 FLIES
18 MONTH

PAGE 22/23

1. D (1 Samuel 17)
2. H (Genesis 12)
3. A (Judges 4)
4. F (2 Corinthians 6)
5. I (Acts 9)
6. J (Esther 4)
7. B (Exodus 3)
8. G (Matthew 1)
9. C (Mark 1)
10. E (Jonah 1)

ANSWERS

PAGE 24/25

S	N	I	P	S		D	A	S	H		S	L	E	D
L	A	D	E	N		I	S	L	E		B	E	M	A
O	P	E	R	A		E	T	U	I		E	V	I	L
B	E	A	S	T	S		E	G	G	S		E	L	I
		I	C	I	E	R		H	O	M	E	Y		
A	B	R	A	H	A	M			T	W	O			
B	O	O			M	O	S	E	S		A	D	A	M
E	R	M	A			T	O	T			B	E	B	E
L	E	E	R		J	E	S	U	S		A	B	S	
			E	G	O		D	E	B	O	R	A	H	
	I	S	A	A	C		C	E	L	L	S			
P	T	A		B	U	R	R		L	U	M	B	E	R
L	A	N	D		L	O	O	P		F	I	O	N	A
O	L	E	O		A	L	S	O		F	U	N	D	S
T	Y	R	E		R	E	S	T		S	M	A	S	H

PAGE 28/29

1. Eve's sheaves
2. Luke's dukes
3. Noah's boas
4. Ruth's booths
5. Aaron's herons
6. Mark's parks
7. Paul's stalls
8. John's fawns
9. Lot's tots
10. Saul's malls

PAGE 26/27

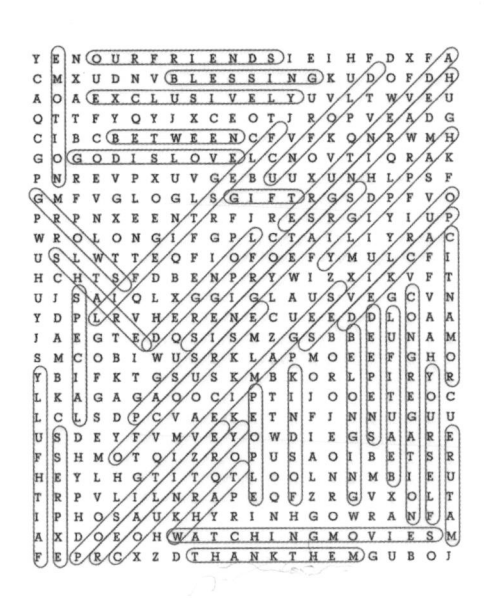

PAGE 30/31

1. J
2. L
3. A
4. F
5. H
6. B
7. D
8. I
9. E
10. C
11. G
12. K

PAGE 32/33

1. A 2. C 3. B 4. C 5. B 6. A 7. B 8. C 9. B 10. A

PAGE 34/35

F	A	C	T			A	C	A	D
A	L	O	O	F		D	O	N	E
M	A	M	M	A		D	A	D	A
E	S	E		T	B		T	E	N
			K	H	A	K	I	S	
	W	I	S	E	L	Y			
D	I	V		R	I		D	A	R
E	V	I	L		N	O	I	S	E
J	E	E	P		G	I	V	E	N
A	S	S	N			L	E	A	D

PAGE 36/37

1. CARNATION 2. DAFFODIL 3. GLADIOLUS
4. SNAPDRAGON 5. PANSY 6. AZALEA
7. DAHLIA   Answer: DAISIES

PAGE 38/39

1. Mi**les sen**sed that **Mary's word**s were t**rue**.
2. Char**lie says he** met **an**other **neigh**bor.
3. Who'**s to ve**nture **d**own this **path**?
4. Are **we d**riving eas**t or n**orth, or are **we re**ally lost?
5. W**ho ot**her t**han G**ary owns a **farm**?
6. I'**m in t**he middle o**f a st**artling pre**sent**ation, c**an't you t**ell?
7. His da**d read** an ad**vent**ure sto**ry e**very **even**ing.
8. No **quest**ion, her f**acts** sur**prise**d us.
9. I'm th**ink**ing An**drew** crawl**ed th**r**ough** the a**venue**.

171

ANSWERS

PAGE 40/41

```
        M A J O R
              V
      W O N D E R F U L
    G   U T   R       A
    I   T D   P       V
  B V   D   G E N E R O U S
  E N E R O U S   E   S
  N   D     D     N   H
  E   E X P E C T Y
V A S T   F R U I T   Y
  H     I     L       B
  B O U N T Y   I   G I V E
  W     S     V   R     S
B E   H   C R E A M   R E A P T
L A R G E               C
E S   A       C O N T E N T
S S   P R A Y         I
          H           C
        S U R P R I S E D
          V         T
          H E L P S
          S
        G I F T
```

PAGE 42/43

1. B
2. A
3. B
4. C
5. A
6. A
7. C
8. A
9. B
10. B
11. C
12. A

PAGE 44/45

S	1. sheets	2. these	3. thee	S
U	4. mouse	5. some	6. ose	M
N	7. sprain	8. pairs	9. spar	I
N	10. lemon	11. mole	12. Moe	L
Y	13. teary	14. rate	15. tar	E

PAGE 46/47

1. Fine 2. Sole 3. Well 4. Fair 5. Bow 6. Lead 7. Ground
8. Tip 9. Desert 10. Wind 11. Rose 12. Bolted 13. Row
14. Duck 15. Board 16. Jam 17. Resume

PAGE 48/49

		A	R	M		
		D	U	O		
		A	G	O		
H	O	U	R		N	E	S	S
U	R	N				Y	E	A
T	E	E	N		N	E	E	D
		O	N	E		
		V	O	W		
		A	R	T		

PAGE 50/51

1. C
2. A
3. C
4. A
5. C
6. A
7. B
8. B
9. A
10. C

PAGE 52/53

O	M	A	H	A		C	O	T		A	C	P
L	A	S	E	R		R	A	H		L	Y	E
E	T	H	I	C		E	R	R		O	C	T
			S	H	O	W		O	V	U	L	E
B	A	T	T	E	R		S	N	I	D	E	R
A	D	D		R	A	C	K	E	T			
T	O	S	S		C	U	E		A	L	I	F
			H	O	L	D	T	O		A	C	E
K	A	R	A	T	E		C	L	A	W	E	D
N	E	I	G	H		W	H	I	R			
U	S	S		E	P	A		V	E	I	N	S
R	O	E		R	E	F		E	N	N	U	I
L	P	N		S	A	T		R	A	N	T	S

PAGE 54/55

1. F (Matthew 14:24-25) 2. H (Luke 23:44-46) 3. B (Genesis 7:12)
4. J (Joshua 10:13) 5. A (Acts (Acts 2:2-4) 6. C (Exodus 10:13-20)
7. D (1 Kings 19:11-12) 8. G (Matthew 28:2-6) 9. E (Jonah 4:6-8)
10. I (Isaiah 58:11)

ANSWERS

PAGE 56/57

1. Think clearly
2. Research
3. Objectivity
4. Discernment
5. Root cause
6. Planning

Answer:
PRAYER

PAGE 58/59

PAGE 60/61

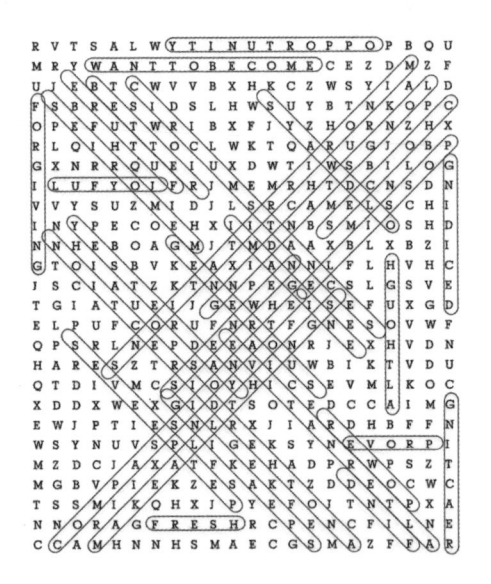

PAGE 62/63

1. E
2. H
3. A
4. F
5. B
6. J
7. D
8. C
9. G
10. I

PAGE 64/65

¹P	²H	³D	■	⁴P	⁵A	⁶T	⁷H	■	⁸A	⁹B	¹⁰S
¹¹R	I	O	■	¹²O	G	R	E	■	¹³S	T	O	P
¹⁴O	F	T	■	¹⁵I	R	O	N	■	¹⁶C	H	A	R
¹⁷F	I	S	¹⁸H	N	E	T	■	¹⁹S	A	L	T	Y
■	■	■	²⁰U	T	E	■	²¹B	A	B	E	■	■
²²O	²³C	²⁴H	R	E	■	²⁵P	O	P	■	²⁶T	²⁷A	²⁸P
²⁹B	O	O	T	■	³⁰R	A	W	■	³¹L	I	R	A
³²I	O	U	■	³³O	U	R	■	³⁴M	O	C	K	S
■	■	³⁵S	³⁶H	I	N	■	³⁷J	I	F	■	■	■
³⁸S	³⁹T	E	E	L	■	⁴⁰L	E	A	T	⁴¹H	⁴²E	⁴³R
⁴⁴N	I	C	E	■	⁴⁵B	E	E	S	■	⁴⁶O	W	E
⁴⁷O	R	A	L	■	⁴⁸T	E	R	M	■	⁴⁹S	E	A
⁵⁰W	E	T	■	⁵¹U	R	S	A	■	⁵²E	R	R

PAGE 66/67

1. Open
Under
Even
HANDED

2. Place
Time
One
ANY

3. Burdened
Do
Coat
OVER

4. Free
Less
Giver
CARE

5. Mate
Self
Hired
HELP

6. Looking
Will
Feel
GOOD

7. Stick
Ride
Kill
JOY

8. Belly
Stock
Gas
LAUGHING

PAGE 68/69

1. G 2. A 3. J 4. C 5. H 6. E 7. B 8. F 9. I 10. D

175

ANSWERS

PAGE 70/71

1. Staff laugh
2. Fear cheer
3. Raise praise
4. Can't chant
5. Funny honey
6. Keen teen
7. Grief relief
8. Glad dad
9. Flee glee
10. Jest test
11. Near cheer
12. Smile style
13. Kind mind
14. Bright sight

PAGE 72/73

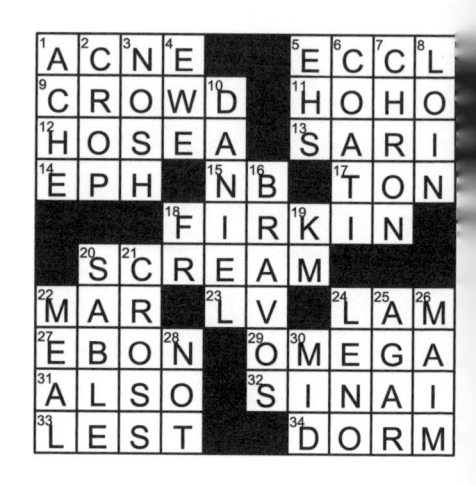

	1	2	3	4		5	6	7	8
	A	C	N	E		E	C	C	L
9	C	R	O	W	D	10	H	O	H	O
12	H	O	S	E	A	13	S	A	R	I
14	E	P	H		15 16 N	B		17 T	O	N
				18 F	I	R	19 K	I	N
	20 21 S	C	R	E	A	M			
22 M	A	R		23 L	V		24 25 L	A	26 M
27 E	B	O	28 N		29 30 O	M	E	G	A
31 A	L	S	O		32 S	I	N	A	I
33 L	E	S	T			34 D	O	R	M

PAGE 74/75

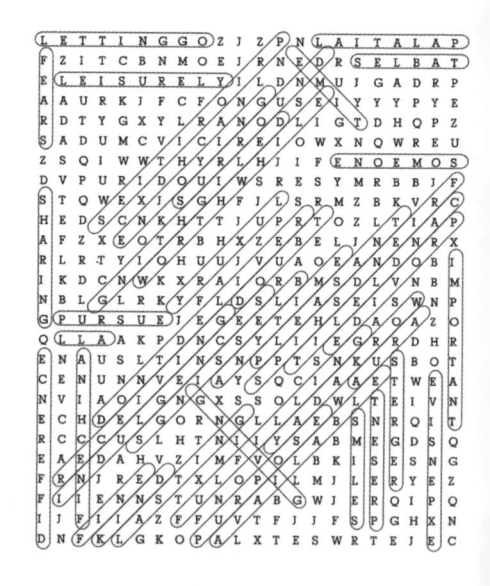

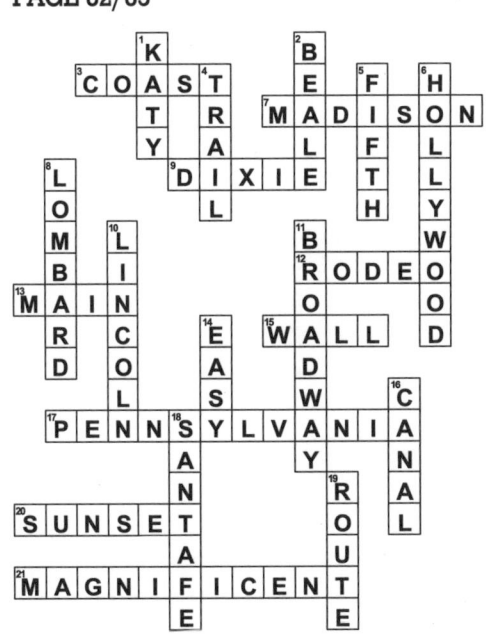

PAGE 76/77

L	1. LAMENT	2. MEANT	3. AMEN	T
I	4. ASPIRE	5. SPARE	6. APSE	R
T	7. TRACES	8. SCARE	9. CARS	E
T	10. BOAST	11. BOAS	12. SOB	A
L	13. TALLER	14. LATER	15. REAL	T
E	16. ESCAPE	17. CAPES	18. PACE	S

PAGE 78/79

Bible verse: I am with you always, even unto the end of the world. (Matthew 28:20)

PAGE 80/81

1. F
2. B
3. H
4. A
5. J
6. C
7. E
8. G
9. I

PAGE 82/83

Across: 3. COAST, 7. MADISON, 9. DIXIE, 12. RODEO, 13. MAIN, 15. WALL, 17. PENNSYLVANIA, 20. SUNSET, 21. MAGNIFICENT

Down: 1. KATY, 2. BEL, 4. TRAIL, 5. FIFTH, 6. HOLLYWOOD, 8. LOMBARD, 10. LINCOLN, 11. BROADWAY, 14. EAST, 16. CANAL, 18. SYLVANIA, 19. ROUTE

ANSWERS

ANSWERS

PAGE 84/85

1. "Roll **over**, Fi**do**!" **ur**ged my **neigh**bor as the e**bull**ient puppy compli
2. He p**lay**ed the ac**cord**ion a**t our** fall **fest**ival this y**ear**.
3. The lu**minescent port**rait ar**rest**ed ou**r at**tention.
4. **If use**ful, ex**pend**itures **can** extend in**to nex**t week.
5. Take a **different** r**out**e **so y**ou get bac**k in** time.
6. Is the te**st over** yet, and did Pete**r ace** it a**gain**?
7. He d**rift**ed from o**ne ar**ea to ano**the**r befo**re findin**g his place.
8. Wa**s layered** cake en**tire**ly ea**ten**?
9. The d**airy** include**d a descript**ion of her **care**er.

PAGE 86/87

D	E	E	R		R	A	G	S
O	P	T	I	C	U	T	A	H
T	E	N	O	R	N	A	M	E
S	E	A		E	D		L	E	D
		R	A	I	S	E	S	
	G	U	I	T	A	R		
P	A	L		E	L		C	A	P
O	U	T	S		O	P	I	N	E
E	Z	R	A		G	H	A	N	A
M	E	A	N			D	O	E	S

PAGE 88/89

1. C (1 Samuel 1) 2. G (Genesis 18) 3. I (Acts 7)
4. A (2 Corinthians 12) 5. D (Exodus 14) 6. J (Psalm 51)
7. H (Matthew 8) 8. E (1 Kings 3) 9. B (Luke 8) 10. F (Luke 15)

PAGE 90/91

1. My thoughts are **not** your thoughts, neither are your **ways** my **ways**, saith the Lord. (Isaiah 55:8)

2. Whatsoever things are true, whatsoever things are **honest**, whatsoever things are just, whatsoever things are pure, whatsoever things are lovely, whatsoever things are of good **report**; if there be any **virtue**, and if there be **any** praise, think on these things. (Philippians 4:8)

3. I know the thoughts that I think **toward** you, saith the Lord, thoughts of peace, and not of **evil**, to **give** you an expected end. (Jeremiah 29:11)

4. The **counsel** of the Lord standeth forever, the thoughts of his heart to all **generations**. (Psalm 33:11)

5. **Which** of you with taking **thought** can add to his stature **one** cubit? (Luke 12:25)

6. A person may think their own ways are **right**, but the Lord **weighs** the heart. (Proverbs 21:2 NIV)

7. His **delight** is in the law of the Lord; and in his law doth he **meditate** day and **night**. (Psalm 1:2)

8. If you think you are standing **firm**, be **careful** that you don't **fall**! (1 Corinthians 10:12 NIV)

9. **Search** me, O God, and know my **heart**: try me, and know **my** thoughts. (Psalm 139:23)

10. **Commit** thy **works** unto the Lord, and thy thoughts shall be **established**. (Proverbs 16:3)

11. The word of God...is a **discerner** of the thoughts and **intents** of the heart. (Hebrews 4:12)

12. Jesus **knew** what they were **thinking** and asked, "Why are you thinking these **things** in your **hearts**?" (Luke 5:22 NIV)

PAGE 92/93

1 VALUE
2 JOY
3 WONDER
4 TRUST
5 FUN
5 FAMILY
6 LOYALTY
7 BLISS
8 MEMORIES
9 DELIGHT
10 LOVE
11 FRIENDS
12 SMILE
13 PURPOSE
14 IMAGINATION
15 PRAYER
16 FAITH
17 PLEASURE
18 OPTIMISM
19 SERENITY
20 HOPE
21 DREAMS
22 HAPPINESS
23 AWE
24 GOODTIMES
25 BEAUTY

PAGE 94/95

Possible solutions:

1. HURT
hart
halt
hale
bale
balm
CALM

2. FEAR
tear
team
tram
pram
PRAY

3. STAY
slay
flay
fray
frat
fret
FREE

4. REAL
teal
tell
till
tile
rile
rife
LIFE

5. TRUE
tree
free
fret
feet
fest
lest
lost
lose
LOVE

PAGE 96/97

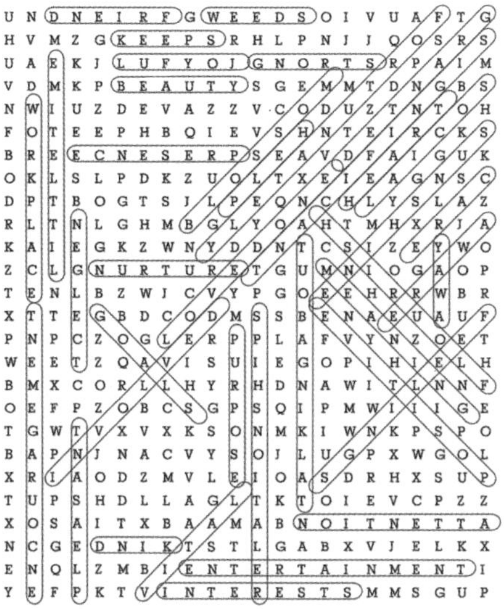

PAGE 98/99

1. B. 2. A. 3. C. 4. C. 5. B. 6. C. 7. A. 8. C. 9. A. 10. B.

PAGE 100/101

1. Moses 2. Hezekiah 3. Gideon 4. Rebekah 5. Paul
6. Sarah 7. Martha 8. Jairus 9. Bartimaeus 10. Jabez
11. Thief on the cross 12. Elijah

PAGE 102/103

A	V	O	W	S		P	E	R	U		B	E	N
F	I	N	I	T	E		A	L	A	S		R	U	E
C	A	E	S	A	R		S	U	R	F		O	C	T
			D	I	R	T		D	E	L	I	G	H	T
	G	O	O	D		U	S	E	R		D	A	R	E
H	A	R	M		G	L	A	D		B	O	N	E	D
A	L	A		F	A	S	T		D	E	L			
M	A	L	A	R	I	A		P	O	S	S	E	S	S
			S	E	T		T	R	O	T		E	L	K
S	T	A	K	E		A	L	A	R		P	L	A	Y
H	O	M	E		D	I	C	T		H	A	S	P	
A	R	T	W	O	R	K		E	Y	E	S			
S	I	R		W	E	I	R		E	A	S	T	E	R
T	E	A		N	A	D	A		T	R	E	A	T	Y
A	S	K		S	M	O	G		T	R	U	C	E	

PAGE 104/105

G	1. GRASP	2. SPAR	3. RAP	S
A	4. PRAISES	5. SPIRES	6. PRESS	I
Z	7. GRAZED	8. GRADE	9. DARE	G
E	10. THINE	11. THIN	12. NIT	H
S	13. STARE	14. RATE	15. ERA	T

PAGE 106/107

1. D. 2. G. 3. J. 4. F. 5. B. 6. I. 7. E. 8. A. 9. H. 10. C.

PAGE 108/109

1. B. 2. B. 3. A. 4. B. 5. C. 6. A. 7. B. 8. A. 9. A. 10. C.

PAGE 110/111

1. TEAM BEAM 2. GRACE PLACE 3. BLISS KISS
4. SMILE STYLE 5. NEW VIEW 6. SWEET RETREAT
7. SMART HEART 8. DEVOUT SHOUT
9. FINE SHINE 10. WINK LINK

PAGE 112/113

G	N	A	W		H	U	B	S
N	A	B	O	B		A	S	E	A
A	M	B	E	R		S	U	I	T
T	E	A		O	W		A	G	E
			I	N	H	A	L	E	
	M	A	T	Z	O	S		
M	C	G		E	L		H	U	E
E	C	R	U		E	B	O	N	Y
N	O	E	S		S	L	A	T	E
D	Y	E	S		T	R	O	D

PAGE 114/115

1. **Her mit**tens we**re daring**ly wor**n in th**e ho**use**.
2. When **we st**ay in t**own, Er**da asks **to review her entries**.
3. **If it** pleases **him, my** happi**ness is al**ways e**norm**ous.
4. "De**liver me!" sh**e yel**led** as I d**ashed into** her a**part**ment.
5. Ha**s Al Sa**nders rented **it, or** is it pur**chase**d from **the re**po ga**rage**?
6. Wha**t a Lent**en **season! Ly**ing on **E**arl's **ham**mock, **we t**alke**d ab**out e**very**thing.

ANSWERS

PAGE 116/117

1. Ewe 2. Kayak 3. Solos 4. Race car 5. Tenet 6. Level 7. Refer 8. Don't nod 9. Civic 10. Redder 11. Rotator 12. Dump mud

PAGE 118/119

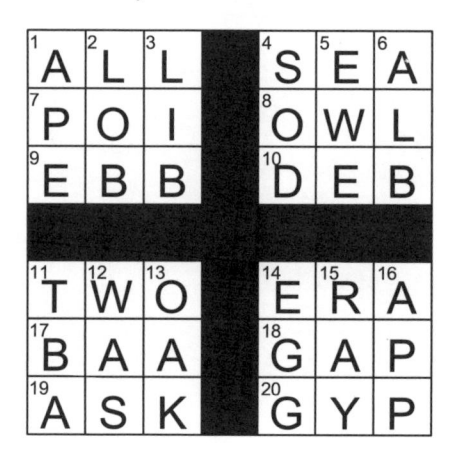

¹A	²L	³L	■	⁴S	⁵E	⁶A
⁷P	O	I	■	⁸O	W	L
⁹E	B	B	■	¹⁰D	E	B
■	■	■	■	■	■	■
¹¹T	¹²W	¹³O	■	¹⁴E	¹⁵R	¹⁶A
¹⁷B	A	A	■	¹⁸G	A	P
¹⁹A	S	K	■	²⁰G	Y	P

PAGE 120/121

1. E.
2. G.
3. A.
4. C.
5. B.
6. H.
7. F.
8. I.
9. F.

PAGE 122/123

¹O	²F	³F	■	⁴S	⁵T	⁶A	⁷G	⁸S	■	⁹W	¹⁰E	¹¹T
¹²R	I	O	■	¹³M	A	N	E	T	■	¹⁴E	A	R
¹⁵E	S	C	■	¹⁶A	R	E	N	A	■	¹⁷A	R	E
¹⁸S	H	I	¹⁹R	R	■	²⁰W	R	I	²¹N	K	L	E
■	■	■	²²E	T	²³A	■	²⁴E	R	A	■	■	■
²⁵E	²⁶M	²⁷B	A	S	S	²⁸Y	■	²⁹S	I	³⁰D	³¹E	³²D
³³M	A	I	D	■	³⁴L	A	³⁵G	■	³⁶V	I	V	A
³⁷U	N	T	I	³⁸E	■	³⁹P	E	⁴⁰T	E	R	E	D
■	■	■	⁴¹E	G	O	■	⁴²L	O	T	■	■	■
⁴⁴D	⁴⁵O	⁴⁶L	D	R	U	⁴⁷M	■	⁴⁸W	E	⁴⁹E	⁵⁰P	⁵¹S
⁵²A	D	O	■	⁵³E	N	O	⁵⁴C	H	■	⁵⁵V	I	A
⁵⁶D	O	C	■	⁵⁷S	C	O	N	E	■	⁵⁸I	L	L
⁵⁹A	R	K	■	⁶⁰S	E	N	S	E	■	⁶¹L	E	T

PAGE 124/125

1. C. 2. F. 3. A. 4. E. 5. I. 6. H. 7. B. 8. G. 9. D. 10. J.

PAGE 126/127

Across: WARM, DARING, FRANK, TRUST, ALERT, LOYAL, CARE, DELIGHT, STEADY, JOYOUS, POLITE, EAGER, WISE, LAUGHTER, KINDNESS

Down: PRUDENT, FAITH, SWEET, GRATITUDE, PATIENT, SMILE, CONTENT, COOL, PAYFUL, TACTFUL, ADVENTURAGE, CULA, HELP, GOVL, ROPE, REST, GIVING

PAGE 128/129

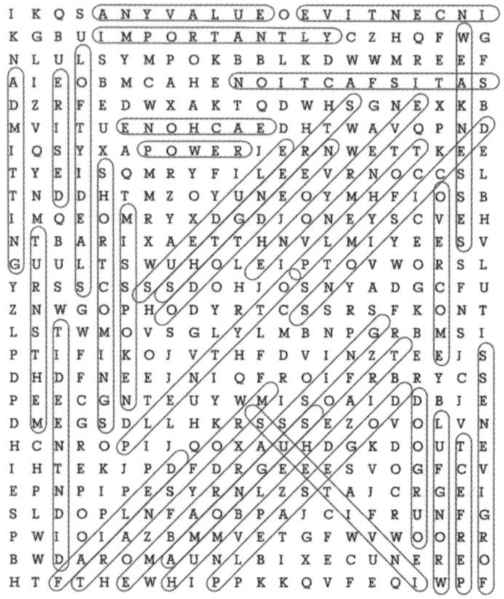

PAGE 130/131

Saying:
Though we travel the world over to find the beautiful, we must carry it with us or we find it not.
Ralph Waldo Emerson

PAGE 132/133

1. H.
2. D.
3. A.
4. I.
5. C.
6. E.
7. F.
8. B.
9. G.

PAGE 134/135

PAGE 136/137

1. Stamp collector: Philatelist
2. Ancestry seeker: Genealogist
3. Code breaker: Cryptologist
4. Coin collector: Numismatist
5. Lettering artist: Calligrapher
6. Bird observer: Ornithologist
7. Beekeeper: Apiarist
8. GPS-armed searcher: Geocacher
9. Cliff descender: Rappeller
10. Book collector: Bibliophile
11. Postcard collector: Deltiologist
12. Music enthusiast: Audiophile

PAGE 138/139

J	1. JOSEPH	2. HOPES	3. SHOE	P
U	4. PUREES	5. SPREE	6. REPS	E
D	7. TENSED	8. TEENS	9. SEEN	T
A	10. AWARE	11. WARE	12. RAW	E
S	13. ASSERT	14. STARE	15. SATE	R

PAGE 140/141

S	H	A	G		E	B	B		S	A	T

(Crossword solution grid)

Across/Down answers filled:
SHAG, EBB, SAT, CARE, PEA, ERIE, OVEN, ADS, NADA, FONTS, LAID, FCA, PSALM, GOT, DRUM, PRONE, MEANIE, PROVEN, URBAN, CRIB, MRS, TALON, TAI, OSLO, TWIGS, ABBR, USS, ABEL, BULB, LEO, VINE, CDT, ADD, EATS

PAGE 142/143

1. A 2. A 3. C 4. B 5. A 6. B 7. C 8. B

PAGE 144/145

1. E 2. C 3. G 4. A 5. H 6. I 7. B 8. F 9. D

PAGE 146/147

1. Serenity 2. Satisfaction 3. Pleasure 4. Enjoyment
5. Fulfillment 6. Achievement 7. Insight
Answer: SUCCESS

PAGE 148/149

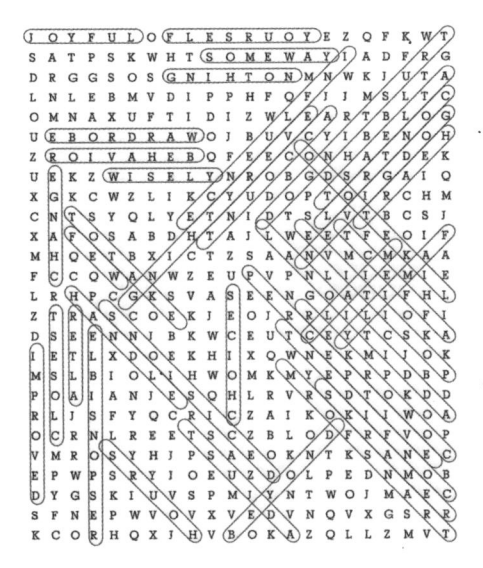

PAGE 150/151

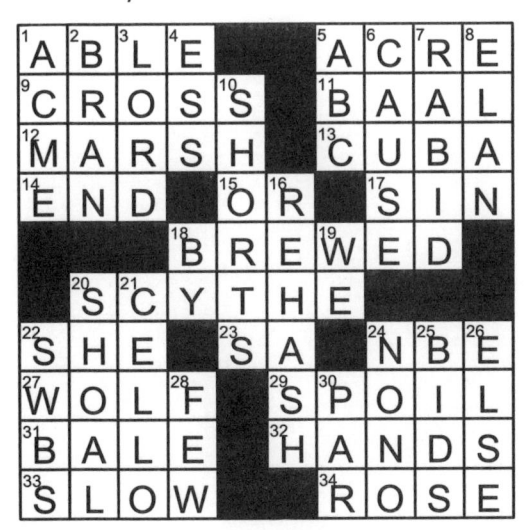

¹A	²B	³L	⁴E			⁵A	⁶C	⁷R	⁸E
⁹C	R	O	S	¹⁰S		¹¹B	A	A	L
¹²M	A	R	S	H		¹³C	U	B	A
¹⁴E	N	D		¹⁵O	¹⁶R		¹⁷S	I	N
			¹⁸B	R	E	¹⁹W	E	D	
	²⁰S	²¹C	Y	T	H	E			
²²S	H	E		²³S	A		²⁴N	²⁵B	²⁶E
²⁷W	O	L	²⁸F		²⁹S	³⁰P	O	I	L
³¹B	A	L	E		³²H	A	N	D	S
³³S	L	O	W			³⁴R	O	S	E

189

ANSWERS

PAGE 152/153

1. HARD
hart
part
port
sort
SOFT

2. MEAN
bean
bead
bend
bind
KIND

3. HATE
pate
path
pith
PITY

4. COLD
cord
word
worm
WARM

5. PAIN
cain
coin
loin
loan
lean
dean
deal
HEAL

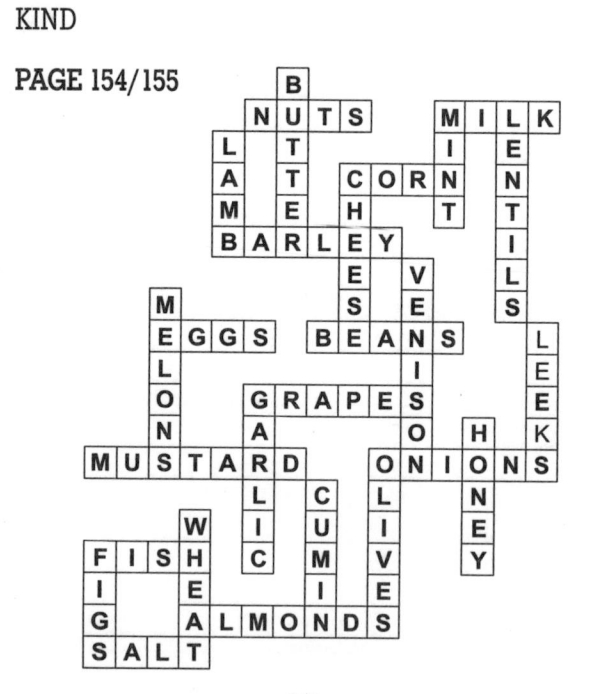

PAGE 154/155

ANSWERS

PAGE 156/157

1. **COMPASS**ION 2. BLES**SING** 3. PER**SEVER**ANCE
4. **OPEN**HANDED 5. AP**PROP**RIATE 6. AMI**CABLE**
7. UNPRE**TENT**IOUS 8. C**OUR**TEOUS 9. CON**SIDE**RATE
10. SUP**PORT**IVE

PAGE 158/159

1. C
2. F
3. I
4. G
5. B
6. D
7. A
8. E
9. H

PAGE 160/161

F	L	A	P		B	I	R	D
L	A	V	A		S	O	L	A	R
E	R	I	C		T	W	I	N	E
A	D	V	I	C	E		A	K	A
			F	R	E	E	D	O	M
P	R	A	Y	E	R	S			
E	E	G		A	S	T	R	O	S
A	C	O	C	K		H	O	P	E
C	U	R	D	S		E	D	E	N
E	R	A	S			R	E	N	T

PAGE 162/163

1. Raven haven 2. Lease peace 3. Grace place or grace space
4. Higher desire 5. Found ground 6. Take break
7. Rest quest 8. Less stress 9. Draw awe 10. Feel Real

PAGE 164/165

1. B (Job 19:25) 2. A (Matthew 5:9) 3. B (John 1:46)
4. C (Acts 9:13) 5. A (Psalm 51:4) 6. B (Luke 2:29)
7. A (Acts 5:38-39 niv)

COUNTING YOUR BLESSINGS

"In every thing give thanks", the book of Thessalonians reminds us. When we count our blessings, and not our problems, we find that our blessings far outnumber the problems, and the problems that exist become less burdensome. Seeing every day through the eyes of gratitude gives new perspective, hope, and joy, to life.

Dear God, open my eyes to see every day with a thankful heart.

Blessings to you as you create your own gratitude list!